Testing in Scala

Daniel Hinojosa

O'REILLY®

Beijing · Cambridge · Farnham · Köln · Sebastopol · Tokyo

Testing in Scala

by Daniel Hinojosa

Published by O'Reilly Media, Inc., 1005 Gravenstein Highway North, Sebastopol, CA 95472.

O'Reilly books may be purchased for educational, business, or sales promotional use. Online editions are also available for most titles (*http://my.safaribooksonline.com*). For more information, contact our corporate/institutional sales department: 800-998-9938 or *corporate@oreilly.com*.

Editors: Andy Oram and Maria Gulick	**Copyeditor:** Rebecca Freed
Production Editor: Christopher Hearse	**Cover Designer:** Randy Comer
	Interior Designer: David Futato
	Illustrator: Rebecca Demarest

January 2013:   First Edition

Revision History for the First Edition:

2013-01-23   First release

See *http://oreilly.com/catalog/errata.csp?isbn=9781449315115* for release details.

ISBN: 978-1-449-31511-5

[LSI]

Table of Contents

Preface

This book started off as a magazine article for a popular conference, No Fluff, Just Stuff (*http://www.nofluffjuststuff.com/home/main*). The article became a presentation, then the presentation became a book. It became evident early on that Scala had something good going on when it came to testing—not only with its variety of quality open source software, but also with automated test generation.

This book revolves around music, albums, artists, and bands. It makes the topics less dry, even though testing is wonderfully exciting, and it includes music from different generations. So anyone alive today will likely encounter a band or an artist that they will like. Music is universal, and relatable to most people. Using music in techical books as examples is not new: two of my favorite O'Reilly titles, Hibernate: A Developer's Notebook and Learning the bash Shell, 3rd Edition used music in some of the examples, and I loved the idea so much I use it in constantly in teaching, in speaking, and of course in writing.

Much of the production code is simple—some might say pedestrian. The intent of the book is not to impress with overly fanciful or verbose production code, but to focus on testing code. As for the testing code, I also try to keep that simple, but I always provide some extra explanation if the code becomes unfamiliar or esoteric.

Audience

This book assumes some Scala knowledge, but recognizes that readers might not know all the nooks and crannies of the language. Therefore, all that is required is basic familiarity. And some Ruby and Python programmers may wander over to learn something different. For those groups, perhaps a quick introduction to Scala is in order. This may be fairly simple for Ruby and Python developers. I believe they are more apt to understand Scala concepts than Java programmers, since many of Scala's language constructs have been used in Ruby and Python for years.

If the reader still does not feel that comfortable with Scala, either visit the Scala website (*http://www.scala-lang.org*) for tutorials, read Dean Wampler and Alex Payne's book, Programming Scala (O'Reilly), peruse the Daily Scala blog (*http://daily-scala.blogspot.com/*) or attend some great conferences, many hosted by O'Reilly, that cover Scala.

Another learning opportunity is learning Scala through Scala Koans (*http://www.scalakoans.org/*). Koans (*http://en.wikipedia.org/wiki/K%C5%8Dan*) are small, Zen-like interactive lessons, meant to foster learning without overwhelming detail. Each lesson is short and comes with its own bite-sized epiphany. New koans are added all the time, and is a fantastic way to learn the language. The koans by yourself which is the lonely way to go, or at a local conference where it is interactive and conducive to more questions and answers.

Organization of This Book

Chapter 1, Setup

> This chapter is about setting up a sample project to be used in the book.

Chapter 2, Structure and Configuration of Simple Build Tool (SBT)

> This chapter consists of a slightly deeper introduction to Simple Build Tool, an open source, Scala based tool and competitor to `ant`, `maven`, and `gradle`. This chapter covers basic commands, using interactive mode, packaging, and using SBT's history.

Chapter 3, ScalaTest

> This chapter shows how to use ScalaTest both on the command line and with SBT. The chapter covers how to use the different specifications, how to tag tests, how to use `MustMatchers` and `ShouldMatchers` domain-specific languages (DSLs), and how to incorporate some of the popular Java-based frameworks, like JUnit and TestNG. This chapters also covers strategies for creating test fixtures with ScalaTest.

Chapter 4, Specs2

> Specs2 is an alternative testing framework that covers its two styles of specifications, unit and acceptance. This chapter delves into its own matcher DSLs, how to use data tables, and how to tag tests. The chapter also covers its own strategies for creating test fixtures with Specs2.

Chapter 5, Mocking

> This chapter covers mocking, the art of substituting large subsystems with objects rehearsed to perform your will to make Scala unit tests isolated. This chapter covers

the Java mocking frameworks EasyMock and Mockito, and how they interact with Scala. This chapter will also cover how to use ScalaTest's sugar to incorporate Easy-Mock with ScalaTest, and how to use Specs2 sugars with Mockito. Finally, this chapter covers a home-grown mocking framework called ScalaMock, which supports mocking for some of the toughest constructs to mock—like functions, companion and singleton objects, and final classes and methods.

Chapter 6, ScalaCheck

This chapter covers an amazing tool that generates fake data for tests and does so thoroughly by creating a set of fake data for tests. This chapter covers how to manipulate ScalaCheck to give you the test data needed for effective unit testing. Finally, the chapter wraps up by showing some ScalaCheck sugars that are available in ScalaTest and Specs2.

About the Book

This book enhances the Scala language with standard test-driven development practices, highlighting the best testing tools today. This book will cover both the ScalaTest and the Specs2 testing frameworks, which help you create quick and easy tests. Testing is also often the most overlooked aspect of introductory programming language books. This book is dedicated to mending that gap.

We will run all these tests using Simple Build Tool (SBT). SBT is similar to some earlier build tools and competitors: Maven, Gradle, and Buildr. What makes SBT highly attractive is its ease of use and the small size of the build file. Type a few lines of code for your build file and you're off and running on your project. We will also cover SBT's wonderful triggered execution feature, which complements test-driven development by building and testing code whenever a file is saved.

ScalaTest and Specs2 are two of the most dominant testing frameworks for Scala around today. Each framework has a different intent and goal, but they share the same ideal of making testing concise, and they both leverage the Scala programming language to make testing easy and fun. Testing frameworks are nothing new, of course, and have been used with other programming languages for years. Those familiar with other programming languages and their testing tools will find some similarities with Scala's current testing tools. ScalaTest and Specs2 borrowed ideas from Cucumber. But upon these shoulders of giants, Scala testing systems have also stepped out on their own and created some of the most mind-blowing testing tools found in any language.

Testing in Scala will also illustrate mocking code, so as to keep our tests isolated from large subsystems and networks. Mocking is, in essence, creating a substitute for various objects to isolate tests from volatile elements of their environment (such as the contents of databases) and to help unit tests run fast. This book shows how you can use Scala with Java-based mocking frameworks that have been used for years by Java programmers, EasyMock and Mockito. We will also introduce you to a new framework, ScalaMock. Formerly known as Borachio, ScalaMock was inspired by Java's EasyMock and Mockito but takes their work further, even offering support for mocking final classes and Scala objects.

Following mocking, we will also generate a massive battery of prefabricated test data using Scala Check, which is borrowed heavily from the Haskell programmed testing framework called QuickCheck. Scala Check has preconfigured formulas to generate strings, numbers, and other various objects automatically. Scala Check also offers formulas to generate your own custom test objects.

This book will be organized in a TDD fashion: test first, fail; test again, succeed maybe; test again, succeed, and so on.

Because Scala is a deep forest of coding possibilities, my intent is to start on familiar ground, with the imperative programming paradigm, and work our way to the Scala functional programming paradigm, discovering some things about functional programming along the way. I will describe some Scala calls that may be obscure, either to introduce you to some constructs that you may not be familiar with, or as a refresher for those that are familiar with Scala.

All code in this book is compiled using JDK 1.7.0, Scala 2.9.2, SBT 0.11.0, ScalaTest 1.8, Specs2 1.12, ScalaCheck 1.10, and ScalaMock 2.4.

Test-Driven Development

Test-driven development is the art of architecting software by specifying a requirement through a test before writing production code. There are many advantages to writing software in this manner. One is that you define what the software needs to do before setting it down in the program. The methodology gives the developer an idea of what the object should look like and be used for before it is built. This is the same simple idea as having someone hold up a picture for you before you commit any nails to the wall. During this time of reflection, you may decide that picture is the wrong size, the wrong color, too high, or too low. How does this translate to software?

Test-driven development starts with tests, each meant to define a single purpose such as "Write customer data to a database", "Move a sprite to the corner of screen," or "Send out notifications that a meeting registration even has occured." The programmer writes the test using the class in question as if he were a developer using the API. Consider how a user would instantiate the object, etc. What problems would the end user encounter by calling the methods? What errors or exceptions should the end user expect?

The class and its methods don't have to exist when you create the test. In fact, while you're creating the test, you may decide to move methods around, remove them, or add new ones.

After developing the test, create the shell of the class and methods with no body. The point of this exercise is to start the test in a failed state. There is no point to running tests that always succeed even when code is missing or incorrect; you want to make sure a test complains when the code it is testing doesn't work.

Once that has been established, add the data types, variables, and method body required to pass the test. At the first attempt, the test may still not pass; that's OK. Further attempts should yield success. When a successful state has been accomplished, if there is a sense that more supporting methods are needed for the class, add another test, add the method signature without the implementation, make the test fail, and then add the production code to satisfy the test.

The adage "Don't throw good money after bad" also plays an important role in test-driven development. Developing a test may clue you in that the class you're planning to test will be irrelevant or misplaced in the project. The more test-driven development is employed, the more tuned in the developer will be to detecting any "code smell" (*http:// martinfowler.com/bliki/CodeSmell.html*). In the end, don't be afraid to throw it all away if the test and its corresponding production class doesn't pass the smell test.

Another point that programmers often overlook is that unit tests are to be isolated. Unit testing in test-driven development is not meant to test other external dependencies, like networks and databases. Many frameworks and developers will hijack the term "unit testing" to test their code against an application server or other large networks. Testing with other large systems and objects is properly labeled *integration testing* and is generally done after the initial unit testing has been performed. To isolate unit tests from large systems, so you can test code without actually making calls to these large systems, employ mocks and dummies to interact with the subject under test.

After the initial test and production code produce successful results, turn to refactoring. Refactoring is changing the production code to get rid of any duplicate blocks, combine methods that repeat themselves, rename methods and variables to make their names consistent, and move methods between any parent class or move them to each child class element.

During this phase, tests will be used as a guide to alert the developer that the code still works. Refactoring is perhaps the most important reason why unit testing is so vital. Since there is a harness for the code being written, you can make changes with confidence.

Another benefit to test-driven development is that an organization can separate development teams while they share the same interface. Both teams can agree on certain shared traits and models, and then go off on their own intensive paths where one team implements the trait or interface and the other codes up objects that depend on the trait or interface. For instance, two teams could decide on the methods needed for data access, after which one team creates a data access object (DAO) for an Oracle or a MongoDB datastore, while the other team works on the business methods using the DAO without actually needing a hard-coded DAO to do the work. When both teams are done, all objects can be developed together and tested as an integration test. The beautiful moral to this story is that large systems can be developed with very little waiting.

Test-driven development does take time—a lot of time, since bad habits die hard. From our first "Hello World," programmers have begun with production code. It takes effort to rewire our brains to think in a "test, write, refactor, repeat" mind set. With practice, test-driven development will pay dividends not only in good code, but in malleable code that you can change on a whim.

Test-driven development lets you build only what you need. It is not surprising that after a few test-write-refactor iterations, code becomes reliable and stable—essentially a work of art.

Conventions Used in This Book

The following typographical conventions are used in this book:

Italic
> Indicates new terms, URLs, filenames, and file extensions.

`Constant width`
> Used for program listings, as well as within paragraphs to refer to program elements such as variable or function names, data types, and keywords.

`Constant width bold`
> Shows commands or other text that should be typed literally by the user.

`Constant width italic`
> Shows text that should be replaced with user-supplied values or by values determined by context.

 This icon signifies a tip, suggestion, or general note.

 This icon indicates a warning or caution.

Using Code Examples

This book is here to help you get your job done. In general, if this book includes code examples, you may use the code in this book in your programs and documentation. You do not need to contact us for permission unless you're reproducing a significant portion of the code. For example, writing a program that uses several chunks of code from this book does not require permission. Selling or distributing a CD-ROM of examples from O'Reilly books does require permission. Answering a question by citing this book and quoting example code does not require permission. Incorporating a significant amount of example code from this book into your product's documentation does require permission.

We appreciate, but do not require, attribution. An attribution usually includes the title, author, publisher, and ISBN. For example: "*Testing in Scala* by Daniel Hinojosa (O'Reilly). Copyright 2013 Daniel Hinojosa, 978-1-449-31511-5."

If you feel your use of code examples falls outside fair use or the permission given above, feel free to contact us at *permissions@oreilly.com*.

 Safari Books Online is an on-demand digital library that delivers expert content in both book and video form from the world's leading authors in technology and business.

Technology professionals, software developers, web designers, and business and creative professionals use Safari Books Online as their primary resource for research, problem solving, learning, and certification training.

Safari Books Online offers a range of product mixes and pricing programs for organizations, government agencies, and individuals. Subscribers have access to thousands of books, training videos, and prepublication manuscripts in one fully searchable database from publishers like O'Reilly Media, Prentice Hall Professional, Addison-Wesley Professional, Microsoft Press, Sams, Que, Peachpit Press, Focal Press, Cisco Press, John Wiley & Sons, Syngress, Morgan Kaufmann, IBM Redbooks, Packt, Adobe Press, FT Press, Apress, Manning, New Riders, McGraw-Hill, Jones & Bartlett, Course Technology, and dozens more. For more information about Safari Books Online, please visit us online.

How to Contact Us

Please address comments and questions concerning this book to the publisher:

O'Reilly Media, Inc.
1005 Gravenstein Highway North
Sebastopol, CA 95472
800-998-9938 (in the United States or Canada)
707-829-0515 (international or local)
707-829-0104 (fax)

We have a web page for this book, where we list errata, examples, and any additional information. You can access this page at *http://oreil.ly/TestingScala*.

To comment or ask technical questions about this book, send email to *bookques tions@oreilly.com*.

For more information about our books, courses, conferences, and news, see our website at *http://www.oreilly.com*.

Find us on Facebook: *http://facebook.com/oreilly*

Follow us on Twitter: *http://twitter.com/oreillymedia*

Watch us on YouTube: *http://www.youtube.com/oreillymedia*

Acknowledgments

Foremost, I would like to thank Dawn Ramirez for everything I can think of.

Additionally, thanks go to O'Reilly and my editors Andy Oram and Maria Stallone, for their editing and guidance with my first book.

My tech reviewers were Bill Venners, Eric Torreborre, Rahul Phulore, and Josh Seureth. Thanks to them for many corrections and suggestions.

Thanks to Mark Harrah for developing SBT; to Bill Venners, Eric Torreborre, Paul Butcher, Cedric Beust, Kent Beck, Erich Gamma, and Rickard Nilsson for their excellent testing products; and to Jay Zimmerman, Venkat Subramaniam, Jared Richardson, Matthew McCullough, and Tim Berglund for networking, inspiration, and a wide range of opportunities.

And for their general support, many thanks go to Ruth Weiner, Kelby Zorgdrager, Bruce Budagher, Michael Budagher, Dianne Marsh, Jason Porter, Kito Mann, Ian Hlavats, Ken Helfer, Dwight Coles, Darold Parker, Gunnar Hillert, Daniel Allen, Mike Arms, Steve Wall, John Ericksen, Robert Engelhardt, Stephen Chin, Marek Novotny, Rodney Russ, Daniel Glauser, and Jeffrey Hulten. Of course family: Mateo Hinojosa, Lydia Hinojosa, Martha Arriola, Jose Arriola, Rosemary Hinojosa, and Hilda Ornelas.

CHAPTER 1

Setup

Simple Build Tool (*https://github.com/harrah/xsbt*) (hereafter called SBT) is a build tool specifically used for Scala projects. SBT uses actual Scala for its build language. SBT runs and compiles Java and Scala files and uses the Maven directory structure. SBT also has a interesting feature called *triggered executions* that will recompile code or run tests whenever you change a file, among other great features. SBT supports multitiered projects and is highly extensible, thanks to its plug-in infrastructure. Just like other build tools, it can package projects and is also extensible by allowing the end user to add more features to the build tool. But unlike other build tools it has a built-in Read-Eval-Print-Loop (REPL) interactive console. The interactive console in SBT can also import a project's class files so that you can experiment with existing project code.

Setup in Mac OS X, Mac OS X Lion, and Linux

Setting up SBT is fairly straightforward. Download the *sbt* JAR file from the website and place it in the *~/bin* directory, which you may have to create in your home directory. Next, create a shell file called *sbt* that will hold the command to launch XSBT:

```
java -jar -Dfile.encoding=UTF8 -Xmx1536M -Xss1M -XX:+CMSClassUnloadingEnabled
    -XX:MaxPermSize=256m `dirname $0`/sbt-launch.jar "$@"
```

Setup in Windows

Setting up SBT in Windows is also straightforward. Create a *.bat* file called *sbt.bat* in a directory of your choosing, and write the following contents there:

```
set SCRIPT_DIR=%~dp0
java -Xmx512M -jar "%SCRIPT_DIR%sbt-launch.jar" %*
```

Next, be sure that your current *.bat* file is located in a directory that is currently mapped to your path in your environment. Depending on your system, add the directory where you placed *sbt* to your path.

For Windows XP, right-click My Computer and then click Properties. Once in the System Properties window, click the Advanced Tab. Click the Environment Variables button. This should bring up the Environment Variables dialog. You will see two sets of environment variables: User Variables and System Variables. User Variables take effect only in your profile, not the entire system. System variables are for system-wide settings. If your account is an Administration account and has full access to your machine, you can add a system variable.

Using SBT

To get started, create a folder for your project. For the project in this book we will create a folder (directory) called *testingscala*. Change into that directory and run the ./sbt program. An Internet connection is required for this step, since some dependencies are required to initialize your directory. When you are finished, you should see the > SBT prompt:

```
$ mkdir testingscala
$ cd testingscala
$ sbt
:: retrieving :: org.scala-tools.sbt#boot-app
    confs: [default]
        1 artifacts copied, 0 already retrieved (838kB/31ms)
Getting Scala 2.9.1 (for sbt)...
:: retrieving :: org.scala-tools.sbt#boot-scala
        confs: [default]
        3 artifacts copied, 0 already retrieved (15178kB/292ms)
Getting org.scala-tools.sbt sbt_2.9.1 0.10.1 ...
:: retrieving :: org.scala-tools.sbt#boot-app
        confs: [default]
        36 artifacts copied, 0 already retrieved (6414kB/103ms)
[info] Set current project to default-362242 (in build file:/home/danno/.sbt/
plugins/)
[info] Set current project to default-cef86a (in build file:/home/danno/
testingscala/)
>
```

Next, type exit at the SBT prompt, since you need to return to your operating system prompt to set up your folder organization and your build file.

SBT Folder Organization

SBT adheres to the Maven standard of folder organization. All source production files go into *src/main* and all test files go into *src/test*. For our small introduction to test-driven development, using Scala tests on Java production code, all we need is a *src/test/scala* directory and a *src/main/java* directory.

The Build File

The build file is a plain Scala file, placed in the root of the project, called *build.sbt*. Here the developer specifies basic attributes such as the project name and version, the Scala version, and all the dependencies required. SBT makes use of the Maven-style repositories to download the binary and source JARs required for your project. One obvious benefit to that procedure is that you never have to commit large JAR file dependencies to your project, since they are automatically downloaded when you run `update`.

Once you have an SBT project ready to go, make sure it uses the latest ScalaTest dependency. In the *build.sbt* file, include your `scalatest` dependency. This will download the `scalatest` library and place it on the `test` classpath automatically.

```
name := "Testing Scala"

version := "1.0"

scalaVersion := "2.9.2"

libraryDependencies += "org.scalatest" %% "scalatest" % "1.8" % "test"
```

`org.scalatest` will look in the maven and scala central repositories by default to look for the dependency `scalatest_2.9.2`. The reason it knows to look for `scala test_2.9.2` and not plain `scalatest` is because the line includes two percent signs `%%` in the address. `%%` will append an underscore and the scala version number to the name of the library. If you don't want SBT to control the scala version and wish to do it yourself, you can specify your own version using `%` instead of `%%`.

Here is the last line of the *build.sbt* file written differently, but accomplishing the same goal.

```
libraryDependencies += "org.scalatest" % "scalatest_2.9.2" % "1.8" % "test"
```

Also note that the declaration consains a scope for our dependency. This would ensure that all classes from this dependency will be loaded only for testing. It will not be used during compilation or packaging.

Now run `reload` within *sbt*, which will compile any *sbt* files, and `update`, which will download and set up the dependencies. At the command prompt, it is possible to call run `sbt reload update` to combine operations. The command will both reload *build.sbt* with the latest changes and update all the dependencies from any repositories.

To run SBT in an interactive shell of its own, run `sbt`, and then do the `reload` and `update` from within the *sbt* console as in the following example.

```
> reload
[info] Set current project to default-ca9689 (in build file:/home/danno
    /development/testingscala/project/plugins/)
[info] Set current project to default-1f0130 (in build file:/home/danno
    /development/testingscala/)
> update
[info] Updating {file:/home/danno/development/testingscala/}default-1f0130...
[info] Done updating.
[success] Total time: 9 s, completed Sep 25, 2011 4:01:06 PM
>
```

That's all it takes to get a fairly simple setup ready for a standard project with testing.

Testing Java using Scala also might give you an excuse to slip some Scala in at work or in your personal projects. Testing in Scala is a great way to learn the language, and if you do it at work in a project you are familiar with, you can see the benefits of Scala in your own domain.

We will place our tests in the *src/test/scala* folder of the project, and we'll eventually place our production code in the *src/main/scala* directory.

About Our Examples

Since this book's focus is on testing, particularly in Scala, I am going to keep the production/target code simple. Don't assume that I'm endorsing the use of TDD just on simple code. TDD is amazing with the most challenging of code, and it's indispensible in times that require some mental clarity and focus.

Our code samples will be a mix of something fun and something relevant. The samples will include a digital jukebox with albums (yes, even in the digital era I still call them albums). Each album will with have an artist associated with it. The artist class will have a band subclass, and each Band will have a collection of artist associated with it. The collections we use for these examples will be the powerful lists, sets, maps, and arrays that come with Scala.

Of course, what good is a digital jukebox without some persistence? Each song will need to persisted into some sort of database, whether it is a classic SQL database or a newfangled NoSQL database. The reason we require an example of storing to a database is because we need it for mocking using a framework such as Mockito, EasyMock, or ScalaMock. If you are unfamiliar with the topic of mocking, you can learn about it in Chapter 5.

Creating Our Examples Using TDD, ScalaTest, and SBT

Let's start SBT triggered execution. Triggered execution in SBT makes TDD exciting and intuitive, since it runs every time there is a change to the code. Because one of TDD's most basic tenets is that unit testing needs to be a constantly repeateable and constantly evolving, SBT will run that test for you without added involvement.

To start triggered execution, run SBT using the command `sbt` on your Mac or Linux box, or `sbt.bat` on your Windows system. If you do so successfully you should receive an `sbt>` prompt. At this prompt, type `~test`. SBT is now listening for your next save. Every time you save a production file, and every time you save your test, SBT will wake up and run your tests again. This is a very nice tool because it keeps your mind focused on your test and your production file. This focused development will not only help you to achieve your goals faster, but will produce a better product in the long run.

We will create our first simple test in the *src/test/scala/com/oreilly/testingscala/* folder, calling the test `AlbumTest`.

 Package folders are a matter of taste. If you want to create a Scala file without the *com*, *oreilly*, and *testingscala* folders, you are certainly free to do so. You can also opt to just have an `AlbumTest` file in the *src/test/scala* folder while keeping the same package name. The choice is up to you and/or your team. All class files will be expanded into their corresponding folders in the *target/scala-2.9.2/test-classes* folder after compilation.

src/test/scala/com/oreilly/testingscala/AlbumTest.scala.

```
package com.oreilly.testingscala

import org.scalatest.FunSpec
import org.scalatest.matchers.ShouldMatchers

class AlbumTest extends FunSpec with ShouldMatchers {
    describe("An Album") {
        it ("can add an Artist object to the album") {
            val album = new Album("Thriller", 1981,
```

```
                    new Artist("Michael", "Jackson"))
        }
    }
}
```

This is a small example of a FunSpec in ScalaTest. We will cover ScalaTest in its own chapter. For this example, FunSpec is a trait, which is a class in Scala that has its own concrete implementation but can be mixed into another class rather like Java interfaces. Our trait FunSpec allows us to think of our test as a behavior-driven test. Behavior-driven development is a refinement on test-driven development. Behavior-driven development provides storied, easy-to-read test reporting to help include other stakeholders such as QA teams in your testing process. When a test has more fluid descriptions of a test, it is also easier to debug since the test-driven developer is able to be expressive and describe the exact intent of the test. When the bug occurs, it is easier to decipher "test that a withdrawal cannot occur when an account has zero funds" than to understand a JUnit-style "testWithdrawalWithZeroFunds." This expressiveness in describing the test is what Dan North, in his introduction to *Behavior Driven Development* (*http://dannorth.net/introducing-bdd*), refers to as bringing the business vocabulary into the codebase.

When you save AlbumTest for the first time, the sbt console shows that SBT's triggered execution ran when you saved changes.

```
> ~test
1. Waiting for source changes... (press enter to interrupt)
[info] Compiling 1 Scala source to /home/danno/testing_scala_book.git
    /testingscala/target/scala-2.9.2/test-classes...
[error] /home/danno/testing_scala_book.git/testingscala/src/test/scala
    /com/oreilly/testingscala/AlbumTest.scala:9: not found: type Album
[error]             val album = new Album("Thriller", 1981,
[error]                                   ^
[error] one error found
[error] {file:/home/danno/testing_scala_book.git/testingscala/}default-cef86a
    /test:compile: Compilation failed
[error] Total time: 1 s, completed Nov 29, 2011 1:35:43 PM
```

Our test failed because we haven't created an Album or Artist class yet. But this is common in test-driven development. We create the test first by creating code that resembles how we want to use the class. Kent Beck in *Test Driven Development: By Example* (*http://www.pearsonhighered.com/educator/product/Test-Driven-Development-By-Example/9780321146533.page*) recommends creating a list of tests before writing code. The point is to first establish the test and make it fail, which we have done successfully.

The next course of action is to satisfy this test to make it pass (maybe). We do so by creating some classes.

src/main/scala/com/oreilly/testingscala/Album.scala.

```
package com.oreilly.testingscala

class Album (val title:String, val year:Int, val artist:Artist)
```

src/main/scala/com/oreilly/testingscala/Artist.scala.

```
package com.oreilly.testingscala

class Artist (val firstName: String, val lastName: String)
```

If you are unfamiliar with Scala, notice that these class declarations are shorter than normal and have and a sprinkle of keywords that you may not be expecting. Also, the variable declarations come before their types are declared. The `val` keyword creates getters for each of the field names, but no setters. Our class in this case is immutable (unable to be changed), which is preferred in Scala, but it is not a hard-and-fast rule. Scala also allows for mutability. For more information about the Scala language and immutability, please refer to *Programming Scala* by Dean Wampler and Alex Payne.

After adding the two classes, when we look at SBT's response we are rewarded with green text (which unfortunately doesn't show up too well if you are reading a black-and-white book). In our response we have an `AlbumTest` one assertion that has passed. We can add `Artist` object to the album.

```
4. Waiting for source changes... (press enter to interrupt)
[info] Compiling 1 Scala source to /home/danno/testing_scala_book.git/testings-
cala/target
    /scala-2.9.2/classes...
[info] Compiling 2 Scala sources to /home/danno/testing_scala_book.git/testings-
cala/target
    /scala-2.9.2/classes...
[info] Compiling 1 Scala source to /home/danno/testing_scala_book.git/testings-
cala/target
    /scala-2.9.2/test-classes...
[info] AlbumTest:
[info] An Album
[info] - can add a Artist object to the album
[info] Passed: : Total 1, Failed 0, Errors 0, Passed 1, Skipped 0
[success] Total time: 4 s, completed Nov 29, 2011 2:18:38 PM
5. Waiting for source changes... (press enter to interrupt)
```

Our result now will show behavior-driven development's storied reporting in plain English: "An album can add an `Artist` object to the album."

The last statement of our triggered executions states that it is waiting for more changes. It also gives you instructions for exiting the triggered execution by pressing Enter. Whenever there is any change to any of the code, the test will run again, giving you the immediate feedback that you need for effective test-driven development.

In the following sections we will cover how to create loads of fake data with ScalaCheck, and how to use mocking within Scala using EasyMock, Mockito, and one of the latest mocking frameworks, ScalaMock, formerly known as Mockito. Later we will cover more about SBT, ScalaTest, and its competitor Specs2. We will cover some gotchas with Scala development, including some of the harder concepts to test such as Scala objects.

Structure and Configuration of Simple Build Tool (SBT)

After the previous chapter, you should know how to create a simple project with Simple Build Tool, or SBT. Obviously there is more to this bleeding-edge utility.

 "Bleeding edge" is the best way to describe SBT. Its 1.0 version is still under development. At the time of writing this book, we are looking at version 0.11.2. This book is authored using version 0.11.0. The differences are immense between the two development versions. Please refer to the wiki (*https://github.com/harrah/xsbt/wiki/*) on github for the latest in SBT.

Directories in SBT

The directories in SBT are styled after the Maven build convention. This avoids confusion and helps any seasoned Java developer to get started with SBT. Run `tree` at your command prompt in project root's *src/* directory (which works across the board on Windows, Linux, and Mac OS X) you can see the folder setup of `sbt`.

The *src* directory has two children, *main* and *test*. *main* is where the production code will reside, and *test* is where the test code will reside. Each of these directories contains a *resources* directory, which contains any dependent files required either by the test or production code. These files can be META-INF configuration files, images, properties, etc.

```
├── src
│   ├── main
│   │   ├── java
│   │   │   └── com
│   │   │       └── oreilly
│   │   │           └── testingscala
│   │   ├── resources
│   │   └── scala
│   │       └── com
│   │           └── oreilly
│   │               └── testingscala
│   │                   ├── Album.scala
│   │                   └── Artist.scala
│   └── test
│       ├── resources
│       └── scala
│           └── com
│               └── oreilly
│                   └── testingscala
│                       └── AlbumTest.scala
```

One thing you may notice about this tree is that we can have two different kinds of production and test files, those written in Scala and those written in Java. If you have a Java production file, place it in the *src/main/java* folder. If you have Scala production file, place that in the *src/main/scala* directory.

 Apologies all around to Windows users, because you probably already know the score, but I should state it formally. Unix, Linux, and Mac OS X users use a forward slash (/) for folder delimiters, whereas Windows users use backslash (\) except for URL resolution.

The *build.sbt* contains the configuration and is placed within the root folder of the project (revisiting the build file from our introduction).

The Importance of Good Infrastructure

An important topic for any new language is the organization of your workspace. This is turn is often determined by the standard tools needed for developing a particular language. C/C++ projects tend not to have a particular folder structure, though a few structures have attained popularity. C/C++ projects are typically built with make, which offers no particular structure (except in the Berkeley version). Ruby projects are often organized according to conventions defined by Rake, the predominant build tool in the Ruby environment.

Java projects originally had no project structure laid out, and developers often thought of different ways to organize source code and compiled code. When the XML-based build tool called Ant came onto the scene, it didn't address how folders should be structured in Java projects, and it allowed developers to continue to go their own way. Then Maven came on to the scene and created and set the standard folder stucture for Java projects. Today, the standard folder structure that Maven first introduced is still used. Since the advent of Maven, other frameworks have come up to the plate to reimagine the programming environment. Gradle is a Groovy-based build tool that compiles and runs Java, Groovy, and Scala projects. Gradle uses the Groovy programming language for its build-tool integrating scripting language as an essential part of the tool. Buildr is another player that uses JRuby to build and run Java, Groovy, and Scala projects. Buildr uses JRuby to define the build script and is structured using very simple tasks without the need for plug-ins. Though they are different in technology, both Gradle and Buildr adhere to the folder structure set by Maven.

And, just like Maven, Gradle, and Buildr, SBT abides by this standardized directory arrangement; however, like its predecessor and its competitors, SBT is written in Scala, including plug-ins. What makes this common infrastucture so important should already be evident. New developers are aware where files will be located—no need to scurry to find source code and JAR files. Since SBT adheres to the infrastructure set by Maven many years ago, it stamps the learning curve down, as most seasoned Java developers can find their way around.

This book will cover SBT because it is actually written in Scala and is becoming the standard build tool for the language for various good reasons.

Triggered Executions

Perhaps one of the most intriguing facets of SBT is the use of triggered executions. Triggered executions are specialized tasks that will run once, display the result of the task, and wait until a file has changed. After a change has been detected it will rerun the task. This in itself makes testing an incredible experience.

The following example encompasses pretty much all you need for a basic SBT file.

build.sbt.

```
name := "Testing Scala"

version := "1.0"

scalaVersion := "2.9.2"

libraryDependencies += "org.scalatest" %% "scalatest" % "1.8" % "test"
```

The name key defines the name of project, "Testing Scala" in this example. The version of our project is 1.0. scalaVersion specifies the Scala version that we want to compile and run our project under. We will see shortly how we can switch the versions of Scala in an ad-hoc fashion and try our code out under different versions of Scala. The lines of the build file must be separated by blank lines.

The last line lists the dependencies required for our project. A *project dependency* is any library that you need for your project to work. There are millions (taking a guess) of repositories out there, but only a few stand out. In fact, depending on what type of project you are working on, the repositories that you use may change. For example, if you are working with the Spring framework (unrelated to this book), you'd likely include a springsource repository in your build file. A later section explains the format of this line.

For dependency management, SBT uses Apache Ivy (*http://ant.apache.org/ivy*), which brings Maven's dependency management system as a product onto its own. Ivy looks up a project's dependency in a repository and downloads them onto the a local repository. The local repository will be located in the user home directory inside of the .ivy2/ cache folder. The purpose of storing dependencies onto a separate location from the project is so that the project can be lightweight with just the source code. No longer will you have to include dependencies in your project and commit them to your version control system, and waiting for that process to complete.

Don't know Git or Github?

Not knowing these is a violation of programmer ethics and punishable by noodle whip! In seriousness: Git is a cross-platform, open source version control system. It is also a *distributed* version control system, so developers can collaborate without a central repository to commit their code to. Every node is a repository, and each repository can share branches and code with each other.

Github is where social networking meets version control. Dare I say… Facebook for programmers. Programmers don't talk about their day, though. They post code to projects, or *gists*. Gists are code snippets pasted on Github used for discussion or just showing off.

Our build file has no repositories to declare, since everything we need will come from either the *maven1* or the Typesafe [1] repositories.

---

1. Typesafe is the company founded by Martin Odersky, inventor of Scala, and Jonas Bonér, inventor of Akka, an amazing messaging stack and memory management software

What If I Need an Extra Repository?

As a Scala developer, you'll probably require a typesafe repository, the main *maven1* repository, or some specialized repository hosted on github (*http://www.github.org*). SBT by default includes the maven central, and typesafe repositories automatically. If you wish to view which repositories are included with SBT, run `view resolvers` and the `sbt` prompt. If you wish to include other repositories in your build, you can add them to the `resolvers` variable of your `build.sbt` file.

```
resolvers += "Codehaus stable repository" at "http://repository.codehaus.org/"
```

In the above sample, resolvers is a sequence of `Resolver` types. `+=` adds the arbitrary name `Codehaus stable repository` and the nonarbitrary URL *http://repository.code-haus.org/* as a repository for SBT to analyze when it requires a library. `+=` is an operator overload that adds a value to a preexisting list of items. We also use this operator when adding dependencies in the next section.

Format of Dependencies Line

In our example build file, we included a dependency in the form of:

```
libraryDependencies += "org.scalatest" %% "scalatest" % "1.8" % "test"
```

Now let's see what that means, piece by piece. `libraryDependencies` is a variable that holds all the dependencies for this project. `+=` is the operator overload that signifies that the dependency we are providing will be added to the library dependencies that have already been established. In the above example, using `+=` assumes that there is already a preexisting list of dependencies—we just wish to add some dependencies to that list.

Now to explain the meaning of the double percent sign `%%`. To start with, the previous example can be written as follows, with just single percent signs:

```
libraryDependencies += "org.scalatest" % "scalatest_2.9.2" % "1.8" % "test"
```

By convention, Scala libraries stored in a repository are named *product__scala-version_*. Suppose, we created a "grande-taco" project and compiled it against Scala versions 2.8.0, 2.9.0, 2.9.1, and 2.9.2. In the repository, you would see the *grande-taco_2.8.0, grande-taco_2.9.0, grande-taco_2.9.1* and *grande-taco_2.9.2* subdirectories.

One benefit of declaring your dependencies with %% is that you can switch Scala versions easily in SBT and it will download the appropriate libraries based on the version of Scala you are using. When your project matures and is ready for packaging and installing onto a repository, SBT can also package and install your project using a list of Scala versions that you declare.

There will be one reason why you may prefer the spelled-out versions with a single % instead of %%. If the Scala version that you are using is not available in the repository, you must supply an explicit dependency instead of one that relies on the Scala version number. For example, if grande-taco is a required dependency and you are using Scala version 2.8.1, but you have not installed a version of the dependency compiled with that Scala version, you will request a nonexistent *grande-taco_2.8.1* and will get an unresolved dependency error. If you have a hard dependency replacement, you may decide to use the explicit address.

```
libraryDependencies += "org.grande-taco" % "grande-taco_2.9.2" % "1.2" % "test"
```

Updating Changes from the Build File

When you are done adding the necessary dependencies, it's time to reload. Either enter the sbt shell and run reload, or enter *sbt reload* at the command line. In either case, reloading will compile your build files only and verify that they are correct. If there is a problem with your build file, fix the issue and reload it again.

After a successful reload, run update either by entering update at the sbt prompt or by running sbt update at the command line. Updating will download all the dependencies required by your project and will report any issues with the download. If you find that you have entered the dependencies incorrectly, fix any issues, and run the reload and update again.

Where do the dependencies go?
Dependencies by default will be located in your *.ivy2/cache* directory in your home directory. If the dependencies for your project are already downloaded, sbt will use the local versions without resorting to what is infamously called "downloading the Internet."

Bringing Some Sources and Documentation

All open-source libraries have source code; mature libraries have documentation.

If you wish to bring sources and documentation into your project, change your dependency declarations in your *build.sbt*.

```
libraryDependencies += "org.scalatest" % "scalatest_2.9.2" % "1.8" % "test"
    withSources() withJavadocs()
```

withSources() downloads source code for the specific libraries, and withJavadocs() returns the documentation for those dependencies.

Running SBT

You can run SBT from your command prompt (Bash, Zsh, Powershell, or DOS Prompt) or go into SBT interactive mode to run commands from within SBT.

From the Shell

You can run any command from `sbt` from within your shell, by calling a list of tasks as arguments.

```
$sbt clean compile
```

If you wish to run an `sbt` task that requires arguments, you can pass the task and arguments as one using quotation marks:

```
$sbt clean compile "test-only com.oreilly.testingscala.AlbumTest"
```

We'll learn more about test-only later in this chapter.

Interactive Mode

SBT has its own powerful shell from which to run tasks. Perhaps one of the amazing things about SBT interactive mode is that it's a fully functioning shell with tab completion. For example, if you wanted to see all tasks that start with a *t*, you can type *t* at the shell and you'll get a list of tasks that start with *t*:

target	task-temporary-directory	tasks	test
test-frameworks	test-listeners	test-loader	test-only
test-options	test:	this-project	this-project-ref
transitive-classifers	transitive-update	trap-exit	triggered-message

Tab completion in SBT goes beyond tab completion for tasks. It can tab-complete on class names and arguments as well. For example, continuing with our test, if we wish just to test only *com.oreilly.testingscala.AlbumTest*, we merely have to type the first few characters of the test's fully qualified name:

```
>test-only com.
```

and hit the Tab key. The SBT shell then offers the response test classes:

```
--                        com.oreilly.testingscala.AlbumTest
```

The -- is meant for calling our tests with options. We will discuss options in the chapters about ScalaTest and Specs2—Chapter 3 and Chapter 4, respectively.

Basic Tasks

The basic tasks for SBT are very easy to remember, and many of these action names have come historically from Maven. Here is a rundown of some of the basic tasks that you will need for this book, and for basic use of SBT.

compile
> Compiles any of the *src/main/java* and *src/main/scala* files and places the class files in a *target/scala_version/classes* folder in the root of the project, where the Scala version is replaced with the version that Scala is compiled under. Remember that Scala compiles to the same class files as Java, so only one folder is required for the compiled classes.

 Before continuing with the other tasks, a little introduction of the target folder is in order, for those who haven't used Maven or any of its successors, like Buildr, Gradle, and of course SBT. The target folder will contain class files, generated reports, and pretty much any machine-generated artifact that isn't source code. When a clean task is invoked, the target folder by default will be deleted. Do not put any critical file, like a source file or configuration file, into the target folder.

clean
> Removes the target folder containing all compiled and filtered configuration files.

test:compile
> Compiles the test classes in *src/test/java* and *src/test/scala* only and places the class files in *target/scala_version/testclasses* folder.

test
> Runs all the tests. Options can be added to select which tests will actually run.

test-only
> Runs a list of specified tests delimited by a space.

reload
> As we have experienced, compiles our build file with the latest settings.

update
> Downloads any dependencies required for the project.

package
> Creates a JAR file of your classes and places them in the *target/scala_version* directory in a JAR file named for your project.

`package-doc`

Creates a JAR named *project_name_scala_version-project_version-javadoc.jar* with all the scaladoc (*http://www.scala-lang.org/docu/files/tools/scaladoc.html*) and javadoc (*http://www.oracle.com/technetwork/java/javase/documentation/index-jsp-135444.html*) documentation in the *target/scala_version* folder.

`package-src`

Creates a jar named *project_name_scala_version-project_version-src.jar* in the *target/scala_version* folder.

`console-quick`

Does the same thing as `console` with the difference that it runs immediately without compiling any classes with changes. This is beneficial when you want to verify the previous state of your classes.

`console-project`

Runs a console, without any of production classes in the classpath, but with the SBT project classes. This is used for the development of Scala plug-ins.

`test:console` *and* `test:console-quick`

These tasks load not only production classes, but test classes and test dependencies too. This is a great feature because you can play around with some test code before making it a class.

`test:console`

will compile any new classes before running the interpreter, whereas `test:console-quick` will run the interpreter without any compilation.

 At the time of writing this book, SBT contains 246 tasks and settings. If you wish to view all of them, run the `tasks` task. To get help on a task, you can run the task `help` *task-name*. Don't invest too much time in the `help` task, since much of it won't display anything until a later version of SBT arrives with more of those help files filled out. If you want to see what values are set to each of these tasks, run `show` *task-name* to display its current settings.

Using the Scala Interpreter

SBT has an embedded Scala interpreter that can be used to run a few examples, try out ideas, or even engineer some production code. The nice thing about the way SBT does it is that, at your request, it class-loads all your production code, all your testing code, or all your project code with its dependencies. As you can gather, this is an amazing advancement in a build tool!

To run a Scala interpreter within SBT, run the `console` task. This class-loads all your production code and libraries into the interpreter.

```
> console
[info] Compiling 2 Scala sources to /home/danno/testing_scala_book.git
    /testingscala/target/scala-2.9.2/classes...
[info] Starting scala interpreter...
[info]
Welcome to Scala version 2.9.2 (Java HotSpot(TM) 64-Bit Server VM, Java
1.6.0_20).
Type in expressions to have them evaluated.
Type :help for more information.

scala>
```

Within our Scala interpreter we can now import a package from a dependency that we declared in our build file. If, for example, you made Joda-Time [2] a dependency, you could import `org.joda.time` within the Scala interpreter and use it.

```
scala> import org.joda.time._
import org.joda.time._

scala> val dateTime = new DateTime()
dateTime: org.joda.time.DateTime = 2011-12-01T11:26:06.509-07:00
```

Knowing Your History

SBT remembers all the commands you enter and saves them to a cache. The history can be reused even after leaving SBT and restarting it. The history commands shown in Table 2-1 are available.

Table 2-1. History of commands in SBT

Command	Description
!	Show history command help, including commands in this table
!!	Execute the previous command again
!:	Show all previous commands
!:n	Show previous *n* commands
!n	Execute the *n*th command in previous command history (!:)
!-n	Execute the *n*th command before this one
!?string	Execute most recent command that contains *string*

---

2. Joda time is an immutable data/time/chronology library. It can serve as a full replacement of *java.util.Date* and *java.util.Calendar*! It is a library that we will use a lot in this book

Command	Description
`!string`	Execute the previous command that begins with *string*
`!?string`	Execute most recent command that contains *string*

You can quit the console at any time by typing the command `:quit` which will get you back into the `sbt` shell. If you wish to quit the `sbt` shell, merely type *quit*, and you will be returned to your normal Bash, Zsh, Windows, or Powershell shell.

Conclusion

This chapter has only touched the surface of what SBT does. At the time of writing, SBT still has not reached version 1.0, but it has been a fully functional build tool for quite some time. It is constantly evolving with contributions and ideas from the Scala community. SBT may have a slightly higher learning curve than other build tools, but its functionality and speed are well worth the mental investment. Another *interesting* feature is the ability to change Scala versions ad hoc within your project. I deliberately used the word interesting since some voodoo is sometimes needed to ensure that all the dependencies use the correct version. Triggered execution is by far the most valuable feature in SBT (in my opinion), and we will use it throughout the rest of this book.

ScalaTest is a popular testing framework created by programmer Bill Venners specifically for Scala. ScalaTest is an extensive behavior-driven development (BDD) suite with numerous built-in specs, but it also intergrates with some of the classic testing frameworks like JUnit and TestNG. ScalaTest also has two assertion dialects to choose from, depending how you want your test to read. ScalaTest's learning curve is fast, and it runs automatically in the test plug-in installed with SBT.

ScalaTest offers several different flavors of tests. The most basic one is the `FunSpec`, which we used to add an `Artist` to an `Album` in our introduction. It contains a standard storyboard that describes the reason for the existence of the test using a `describe` clause and subsequent tests that fulfill that description. As we saw in our introductory chapter, `AlbumTest.scala` took the form:

```
package com.oreilly.testingscala

import org.scalatest.FunSpec
import org.scalatest.matchers.ShouldMatchers

class AlbumTest extends FunSpec with ShouldMatchers  {
   describe("An Album") {
      it ("can add a Artist object to the album") {
         val album = new Album("Thriller", 1981,
            new Artist("Michael", "Jackson"))
      album.artist.firstName should be ("Michael")
      }
   }
}
```

`AlbumTest` in this example extends `FunSpec`. This is a standard BDD specification. `FunSpec` is a trait, which means that is mixed into a class. This mixed-in trait provides us with a few methods to run our test: `describe` and `it`. `describe` is the subject of the test. In our case we are testing an `Album`, that is subject under specification. Each test is specified using an `it` method, which is mixed in from `FunSpec`.

`it` is used to describe the purpose of the test.

In our example, the `it` method verifies that we can add an `Artist` to an `Album` at construction time.

`AlbumTest` also mixed in the trait `ShouldMatchers`. The `ShouldMatchers` trait provides a DSL used to make the assertions. In `AlbumTest`, the `ShouldMatchers` trait was used to form the assertion:

```
album.artist.firstName should be ("Michael")
```

Note the `should` verb in the statement. The lefthand side of the assertion will typically be the object whose state is being investigated, and the righthand side will typically be the value that is expected. If any matcher fails, the matcher will throw a `Test FailedException`. At that point, ScalaTest will trap that error and report it as a failed test. If the matcher succeeds, nothing happens, and the test continues.

Setting up ScalaTest in SBT

ScalaTest can be run on the command line or through a build tool like SBT, as we have already prepared.

We can run our earlier `AlbumTest` with a command issued within the project folder:

```
$ scala -cp scalatest-1.8.jar org.scalatest.tools.Runner -p . -o -s AlbumTest
```

ScalaTest is meant to be readable at the output, giving a clean, storylike output. If you have terminal coloring, tests that pass will be formatted with the color green, giving you intuitive feedback about the success of your code.

To use ScalaTest in SBT, include the dependency vector in *build.sbt* as described in Chapter 2. For a refresher, either one of these lines will work.

```
libraryDependencies += "org.scalatest" %% "scalatest" % "1.8" % "test"

libraryDependencies += "org.scalatest" % "scalatest_2.9.2" % "1.8" % "test"
```

For information about what each of these settings mean, please refer to Chapter 2.

The next section will discuss the many ways a developer can write assertions using ScalaTest.

Matchers

In the previous example, we made an assertion that the first name of the `Thriller` artist's was indeed `Michael`. These assertions check that the code results in a state that we are expecting.

ScalaTest's assertions come in two flavors: `MustMatchers` and `ShouldMatchers`. The only difference between them is the language that shows up in the testing report.

Types of Matchers

ScalaTest provides a range of matchers for many situations. In the following subsections we'll illustrate them with Should Matchers, because Must Matchers work the same way.

Simple matchers

Simple matchers perform the simple act of asserting one value with another.

src/test/scala/com/oreilly/testingscala/ShouldMatcherSpec.scala.

```
val list = 2 :: 4 :: 5 :: Nil
list.size should be (3)
```

The right hand value that is being evaluated must be enclosed in parentheses. While there is an urge to not use parentheses in the last part of an assertion, it is required. If you miss the parentheses there will be a compilation error. For example `list.size should be 3` is incorrect and will not compile. The assertion should be changed to `list.size should be (3)` in order for it to compile.

The same assertion can be made using the `equal` method:

```
list.size should equal(3)
```

There rarely is any value in asserting a condition using == and != in ScalaTest, because the line will be evaluated but no actual testing assertion will be made. For example, merely stating that `list.size == 4` in the previous example will be evaluated to `false`, but the test will still continue to run and possibly report a successful completion since a `TestFailedException` is not thrown.

String matchers

ScalaTest includes matchers that aid in making assertions about strings. You can determine whether one string contains another, starts with a particular string, ends with a particular string, or matches a regular expression. For more information on regular expressions and how to sculpt them effectively, see *Mastering Regular Expressions* by Jeffrey E.F. Friedl (O'Reilly).

```
val string = """I fell into a burning ring of fire.
        I went down, down, down and the flames went higher"""
```

```
string should startWith("I fell")
string should endWith("higher")
string should not endWith "My favorite friend, the end"
string should include("down, down, down")
string should not include ("Great balls of fire")

string should startWith regex ("I.fel+")
string should endWith regex ("h.{4}r")
string should not endWith regex("\\d{5}")
string should include regex ("flames?")

string should fullyMatch regex ("""I(.|\n|\S)*higher""")
```

These are examples of ScalaTest's string matchers. Using a Johnny Cash lyric, the first assertion checks that this particular lyric starts with "I fell," while the second assertion checks that the lyric ends with the String "higher." The third assertion uses not to assert that Jim Morrison and Johnny Cash lyrics are not mixed. The fourth assertion asserts that indeed the lyrics "down, down, down" are included. The fifth assertion makes sure that Jerry Lee Lewis's lyrics are not included in the *Ring of Fire*, because having *Great Balls of Fire* in *Ring of Fire* might violate a some fire codes in some counties.

The sixth through ninth assertions use regular expressions. The last assertion uses fullyMatch as a modifier to regex to assert that the entire lyric must match the regular expression.

 A keen eye will have noticed that the last assertion uses triple quotes instead of single quotes for the regular expression. This is preferable because in Scala a triple quote, or raw string, saves you from having to escaping each backslash (\) and make it two backslashes (\\). For more information on escaping backslashes and raw strings, refer to *Programming Scala* by Dean Wampler and Alex Payne (O'Reilly).

Relational operator matchers

ScalaTest supports relational operators. These examples should be self-explanatory.

```
val answerToLife = 42
answerToLife should be < (50)
answerToLife should not be > (50)
answerToLife should be > (3)
answerToLife should be <= (100)
answerToLife should be >= (0)
answerToLife should be === (42)
answerToLife should not be === (400)
```

Perhaps the only ScalaTest that requires explanation is the triple-equal operator (===). The operator is used to evaluate whether the right hand side is equal to the left. As mentioned previously, using Scala's equals operator (==) will only evaluate equality, but never assert equality, so it's best to stick with should be, should equal, or ===.

Floating-point-matchers

Floating-point arithmetic in the Java virtual machine (JVM) is a nasty business—worthy of a Discovery Channel reality show.

Consider the operation 0.9 - 0.8. A seasoned Java developer knows that this is not an innocent call. Running that operation in a Scala REPL will result in 0.09999999999999998. ScalaTest provides a buffer to account for some of these inaccuracies using a plusOrMinus method.

```
(0.9 - 0.8) should be (0.1 plusOrMinus .01)
(0.4 + 0.1) should not be (40.00 plusOrMinus .30)
```

In the first line, the righthand side operation asserts that the answer is 0.1 plus or minus a discrepancy of 0.1. The second line in the example is not based much in reality, but just shows that plusOrMinus can be used in any kind of circumstance that you can invent.

Reference matchers

In Scala, a very important point to consider is that the == operator evaluates the natural equality for value types and object identity for reference types, not reference equality. In ScalaTest, the === will assert object equality. But to test object references, ScalaTest offers theSameInstanceAs:

```
val garthBrooks = new Artist("Garth", "Brooks")
val chrisGaines = garthBrooks

garthBrooks should be theSameInstanceAs (chrisGaines)

val debbieHarry = new Artist("Debbie", "Harry")
garthBrooks should not be theSameInstanceAs(debbieHarry)
```

This example will instantiate a new Artist, Garth Brooks—perhaps you'd recognize him as one of your friends in low places. The Garth Brooks object is referenced by the garthBrooks variable, and also by the chrisGaines variable (*http://en.wikipedia.org/ wiki/Chris_Gaines*). The third line asserts that the object the garthBrooks variable is referencing is the same object. The last two lines of the example assert that a Debbie Harry object is not the same object as Garth Brooks. If he is, well, congratulations go out to Garth Brooks for pulling a really nifty trick.

Iterable matchers

For `Iterable`, one of many types in Scala that make up a collection (*http://www.scala-lang.org/api/current/index.html#scala.collection.Iterable*), ScalaTest provides a couple of methods to help you make assertions.

```
List() should be('empty)
8 :: 6 :: 7 :: 5 :: 3 :: 0 :: 9 :: Nil should contain(7)
```

The first line uses an `'empty` Scala symbol to assert that an `Iterable` is empty.

Symbols in Scala are defined as object `scala.Symbol` and are typically used as identifiers and keys. Symbols are immutable placeholders, and unlike strings that are used as a definition or a setting than a String to represent a name, account number, etc.

The second line in the above example asserts that Jenny's number actually contains the number 7 in the `List`.

Seq and traversable matchers

ScalaTest has `length` and `size` matchers to determine the size of a `Seq` or `Traversable`. According to the ScalaDoc (*http://www.scala-lang.org/api/current/index.html#scala.collection.Seq*), `length` and `size` are equivalent, therefore their use depends on your preference.

```
(1 to 9) should have length (9)
(20 to 60 by 2) should have size (21)
```

Map matchers

ScalaTest has a special matcher syntax for `Map`. Assertions with `Map` include the ability to ask whether a key or value is in the `Map`.

```
val map = Map("Jimmy Page" -> "Led Zeppelin", "Sting" -> "The Police",
    "Aimee Mann" -> "Til\' Tuesday")
map should contain key ("Sting")
map should contain value ("Led Zeppelin")
map should not contain key("Brian May")
```

The example is self-explanatory. Given a map of artist names with their associated band names, assertions are made that `Sting` is associated with the `Police` and that `Jimmy Page` is associated with `Led Zeppelin`. The last line, an assertion is made that `Brian May`, guitarist for Queen, is not in the map.

Compound matchers

ScalaTest's `and` and `or` methods can be used to create compound assertions in a test.

```
val redHotChiliPeppers = List("Anthony Kiedis", "Flea", "Chad Smith", "Josh
    Klinghoffer")
redHotChiliPeppers should (contain("Anthony Kiedis") and
    (not contain ("John Frusciante")
    or contain("Dave Navarro")))
```

This example is a list of the current members of the Red Hot Chili Peppers as a List of String objects. The assertion is made that the List contains singer Anthony Kiedis but does not contain former guitarists, John Frusciante and Dave Navarro.

In practice, using compound matchers will pose some difficulty with the parentheses. Here are some rules to keep in mind when engineering compound assertions. First, parentheses must be included around and and or assertions. Secondly, remember that the righthand assertion must also be wrapped in parentheses. The following line would not compile.

```
redHotChiliPeppers should not contain "The Edge" or contain "Kenny G"
```

To fix the first issue, we apply parentheses around the or assertion.

```
redHotChiliPeppers should not (contain "The Edge" or contain "Kenny G")
```

This still will not compile, because we don't have parentheses around the righthand side of the assertions The Edge or Kenny G. After we repair this, the example should look as follows and should compile.

```
redHotChiliPeppers should not (contain ("The Edge") or contain ("Kenny G"))
```

Another rule to keep in mind with compound matchers is that and and or are *not* short-circuited. In other words, all clauses are evaluated even when other languages would decide they are unnecessary and would skip their evaluation. The following example illustrates that rule.

```
var total = 3
redHotChiliPeppers should not (contain ("The Edge") or contain {total += 6;
    "Kenny G"})
total should be (9)
```

The above contrived example will set a var variable to 3. If you are unfamiliar with var, var is a non-final variable with the ability to change the reference[1]. Under short-circuiting in another language such as Lisp or Perl, total would never be increased by 6, because the Red Hot Chili Peppers don't contain The Edge and therefore the first assertion is true. A short-circuiting language would stop and not evaluate the second clause. But since ScalaTest does not short circuit, both clauses are evaluated.

---

1. Everything is treated as an object and an object reference in Scala, but in compiled bytecode all bets are off.

Lastly, Scala rarely deals with null because Scala has Some(...) and None to avoid these cases. But Java uses null, a lot, and since ScalaTest is Java-friendly, there will be circumstances where you care about null when architecting test cases.

```
gorillaz should (not be (null) and contain ("Damon Albarn"))
```

The previous example will generate the ever-so-hated NullPointerException when a developer if gorillaz is referencing null. To avoid this prickly message, undo compound assertions and place each assertion on a line of its own:

```
gorillaz should not be (null)
gorillaz should contain ("Damon Albarn")
```

If gorrillaz is null, the test still won't pass, which is correct. But this time the other test won't throw a NullPointerException.

Property matchers

ScalaTest has also a clever way to assert that an object's properties (found through its getter methods) are valid in one cohesive check.

```
import scala.collection.mutable.WrappedArray
val album = new Album("Blizzard of Ozz", 1980, new Artist("Ozzy", "Osbourne"))
album should have (
    'title ("Blizzard of Ozz"),
    'year (1980),
    'artist (new Artist("Ozzy", "Osbourne"))
)
```

Property matchers can be used to reflect on the object's properties and make assertions on those properties. This example checks that the album *Blizzard of Ozz* was created in 1980 by some chap named Ozzy Osbourne. Assertions can be made to be sure that the title, year, and artist are indeed the ones given at instantiation. It is worth remembering that Artist is a class whose parameters are val, therefore getters are created automatically by Scala and using property assertions will work. It would also work to make all the properties of Artist a var, since var creates both a getter and a setter implicitly.

java.util.Collection matchers

Since ScalaTest is Java friendly, it can be used to make a assertions about basic java.util collections in the same way that it can test Scala collections. The following example shows many of the methods used previously, like should have length, should con tain, etc.

```
import java.util.{List => JList, ArrayList => JArrayList, Map => JMap,
    HashMap => JHashMap}

val jList: JList[Int] = new JArrayList[Int](20)
jList.add(3); jList.add(6); jList.add(9)
```

```
val emptyJList: JList[Int] = new JArrayList[Int]()

emptyJList should be('empty)
jList should have length (3)
jList should have size (3)
jList should contain(6)
jList should not contain (10)

val backupBands: JMap[String, String] = new JHashMap()
backupBands.put("Joan Jett", "Blackhearts")
backupBands.put("Tom Petty", "Heartbreakers")

backupBands should contain key ("Joan Jett")
backupBands should contain value ("Heartbreakers")
backupBands should not contain key("John Lydon")
```

The top line may look esoteric to beginners. Since there is a List container in Scala as well as in Java, Scala provides an import alias that can be used to rename classes used within the class. In the previous example, whenever a java.util.List is required, it will be referred to in the test class as JList. ArrayList will be referred to as JList, Map as JMap, and HashMap as JHashMap.

The first half of the example creates a JList of Int referenced by jList and an empty JList of Int called emptyJList. The following five lines just make an assertion about java.util.List using the same ScalaTest language as for Scala collections. backup Bands is a java.util.Map construct that maps a headliner with the backup band using the same ScalaTest map assertions used for Scala maps.

There is no extra setup or hassle to get ScalaTest to work with "Plain Old Java."

MustMatchers

What is the difference between ShouldMatchers and MustMatchers? Nothing except how you would like the assertion to display on the output. Do not expect that should should pass through, while a must matcher will throw a TestFailedException. If an assertion is not met using either matcher, a TestFailedException will be thrown regardless of whether you use should or must. The following is a small cross-section of all the examples seen in the previous section, except the word should is replace with the word must.

```
val list = 2 :: 4 :: 5 :: Nil
list.size must be(3)

val string = """I fell into a burning ring of fire.
                I went down, down, down and the flames went higher"""
string must startWith regex ("I.fel+")
string must endWith regex ("h.{4}r")
```

```
val answerToLife = 42
answerToLife must be < (50)
answerToLife must not be >(50)

val garthBrooks = new Artist("Garth", "Brooks")
val chrisGaines = garthBrooks
val debbieHarry = new Artist("Debbie", "Harry")
garthBrooks must be theSameInstanceAs (chrisGaines)

(0.9 - 0.8) must be(0.1 plusOrMinus .01)

List() must be('empty)
1 :: 2 :: 3 :: Nil must contain(3)
(1 to 9).toList must have length (9)
(20 to 60 by 2).toList must have size (21)

val map = Map("Jimmy Page" -> "Led Zeppelin", "Sting" -> "The Police",
    "Aimee Mann" -> "Til\' Tuesday")
map must contain key ("Sting")
map must contain value ("Led Zeppelin")
map must not contain key("Brian May")

val redHotChiliPeppers = List("Anthony Kiedis", "Flea", "Chad Smith",
    "Josh Klinghoffer")
redHotChiliPeppers must (contain("Anthony Kiedis") and
  (not contain ("John Frusciante")
    or contain("Dave Navarro")))
```

Exception Handling

There are a couple of ways in ScalaTest to verify that an expected exception is made and trapped. The first way is by placing the volatile code in an intercept block. The intercept block is analogous to the barrels used by bomb sqauds to defuse bombs: any code expected to throw an exception is placed in the block. If the code does *not* throw the expected exception, the test will fail.

```
"An album" should {
  "throw an IllegalArgumentException if there are no acts when created" in {
    intercept[IllegalArgumentException] {
      new Album("The Joy of Listening to Nothing", 1980, List())
    }
  }
}
```

This example is a standard spec that expects an `IllegalArgumentException` when an `Album` is created with no `Artist`. If the instantiation of `Album` does not throw an exception, the test itself will fail.

Another way to assert that an exception should be thrown is to use either a `Should Matcher` or `MustMatcher` to assert that the call indeed throws the necessary `Exception`. This is done using an `evaluating` block and either a `must` or `should` clause to check that it produces the expected `Exception`, as seen in the following example.

```
val thrownException = evaluating {new Album("The Joy of Listening to Nothing",
    1980, List())} must produce [IllegalArgumentException]
thrownException.getMessage() must be ("An Artist is required")
```

The two examples do nearly the same thing, but the second one using the `evaluating` clause allows the developer to introspect the `Exception` and assert information about the exception after it has been thrown. One of the benefits of using this method is that a call often throws different exceptions, and it is good practice to find out exactly which one was thrown. If by chance the class `Album` does has two different cases where an `IllegalArgumentException` is thrown (say, one when there is no `Artist` placed onto the album, and one where the album year is less than 1900) it would be wise to introspect the exception and make sure that the right one was captured. If it isn't, the test should fail. The `evaluating` example just shown does extra analysis to ensure that the `IllegalArgumentException` that is thrown indeed the one that was expected.

Informers

Before continuing further into the different specifications, an introduction to some of the tools available in ScalaTest is in order. We'll start with informers—not the kind that'll rat you out. Informers in ScalaTest are spices, analogous to debug statements, that can be applied anywhere in a test to display information about the test. To apply an informer, merely add an `info(String)` method anywhere within your test.

Informers provide enhanced feedback on the test and give any stakeholder on the project a clear picture of the purpose of your test.

```
class AlbumSpec extends FunSpec with ShouldMatchers {
  describe("An Album") {
    it("can add an Artist to the album at construction time") {
      val album = new Album("Thriller", 1981, new Artist("Michael", "Jackson"))
      info("Making sure that Michael Jackson is indeed the artist of Thriller")
      album.acts.head.asInstanceOf[Artist].firstName should be("Michael")
      album.acts.head.asInstanceOf[Artist].lastName should be("Jackson")
    }
  }
}
```

The testing results will give us the informer's results, prepended with + to denote that the printout comes from an informer. Running `test-only com.oreilly.testingsca la.AlbumSpec` will render the following response in SBT. As a reminder `test-only` takes a test class argument so that SBT will only test one class. In our case that's `com.oreil ly.testingscala.AlbumSpec`.

```
> test-only com.oreilly.testingscala.AlbumSpec
[info] Compiling 1 Scala source to /home/danno/testing_scala_book.git
    /testingscala/target/scala-2.9.2/test-classes...
[info] AlbumSpec:
[info] An Album
```

```
[info] - can add an Artist to the album at construction time
[info]    + Making sure that Michael Jackson is indeed the artist of Thriller
[info] Passed: : Total 1, Failed 0, Errors 0, Passed 1, Skipped 0
[success] Total time: 4 s, completed Dec 19, 2011 11:16:12 AM
```

GivenWhenThen

These are three words any test-driven developer will remember. ScalaTest, as well as Specs2, which will be covered later in the book, uses the three phases to document the scenario and outcome of a test. Just about every process and recipe in the world can be described with GivenWhenThen.

Given we have eggs, milk, flour, sugar, baking powder, and baking soda. When mixed together and placed in an oven of 350°F, then we partake in an opulent cake!

Testing is the same. Each test has a Given that is the initial state of a test. In this initial state we typically gather any nouns or ingredients to the test. Following is a When: which actions or verbs are to be performed on the nouns provided in the Given clause. Finally, Then specifies the results of the test, where all post-action analysis takes place.

The silent partner in the GivenWhenThen trait is the and method. It serves to break apart any given, when, and then if any of those clauses get too unwieldy. It should be visibly evident that a given, when, or then clause has perhaps gotten big if the string describing the test is littered with and+s. For example, if a then clause states that "the act should be an instance of +Artist and the artist's first and last names should be Michael Jackson" it would be better to break the then clause apart, making it both more readable and more logically categorized. For instance: "the act should be an instance of Artist" and "the Artist's first and last names should be Michael Jackson."

GivenWhenThen in the back end are just informers that help the test-driven developer organize her thoughts in a familiar structure. GivenWhenThen is a trait that can be mixed into any test. This is particularly useful for a Spec that doesn't have a strict structure.

GivenWhenThen can therefore be applied anywhere where needed. The technique goes particularly well with FunSpec, ["FunSpec" (page 36)] and FeatureSpec, ["FeatureSpec" (page 40)].

The following example retrofits the Album test, mixing in GivenWhenThen methods.

```
class AlbumSpec extends FunSpec with ShouldMatchers with GivenWhenThen {
  describe("An Album") {
    it("can add an Artist to the album at construction time") {
      given("The album Thriller by Michael Jackson")
      val album = new Album("Thriller", 1981, new Artist("Michael", "Jackson"))

      when("the album\'s artist is obtained")
      val artist = album.artist
```

```
    then("the artist obtained should be an instance of Artist")
    artist.isInstanceOf[Artist] should be (true)

    and("the artist's first name and last name should be Michael Jackson")
    artist.firstName should be("Michael")
    artist.lastName should be("Jackson")
    }
  }
}
```

Pending Tests

Each test trait lets you mark a test as pending. pending is a placeholder for tests that
have not been defined. The benefit of pending is that it lets you quickly jot down an
idea, perhaps something that popped into your mind while you were focused on something else. pending also is a great way to map out a course of tests before actual implementation, possibly eliminating some ideas that you thought would make sense at first
but didn't after delineating the purpose of all the tests.

In a Spec, after each it clause the corresponding block returns pending for any test that
is not implemented or just not ready.

When I first had the idea for AlbumTest and was jotting down possible tests to include,
pending might have made the test look like the following:

```
class AlbumSpec extends FunSpec with ShouldMatchers with GivenWhenThen {
  describe("An Album") {
    it("can add an Artist to the album at construction time") {pending}
    it("can add opt to not have any artists at construction time") {pending}
  }
}
```

The tests marked as pending will generate output marked pending when run either at
the command prompt or through SBT.

```
[info] AlbumSpec:
[info] An Album
[info] - can add an Artist to the album at construction time (pending)
[info] - can add opt to not have any artists at construction time (pending)
```

An interesting use of pending is to keep that keyword on the bottom of the test while
implementing it, so that the test is still considered under construction. When the test is
ready, let it run by removing the pending statement.

```
class AlbumSpec extends FunSpec with ShouldMatchers {
  describe("An Album") {
    it("can add an Artist to the album at construction time") {
      val album = new Album("Thriller", 1981, new Artist("Michael", "Jackson"))
      info("Making sure that Michael Jackson is indeed the artist of Thriller")
```

```
        pending
    }

    it("can add opt to not have any artists at construction time") {pending}
  }
}
```

This example is a test still in progress. As long as the test compiles, you can run it through ScalaTest and the last `pending` guarantees that the test runner will still treat this as a pending test. ScalaTest will not cruelly discipline the test-driven developer with failures for an incomplete test. Note that the previous example also contains an informer that is rendered in the test results, as seen below, even though the test is pending. If the test is marked as `pending`, ScalaTest will still honor any informers, including `GivenWhenTh` `en` methods.

```
[info] AlbumSpec:
[info] An Album
[info] - can add an Artist to the album at construction time (pending)
[info]    + Making sure that Michael Jackson is indeed the artist of Thriller
[info] - can add opt to not have any artists at construction time (pending)
```

Ignoring Tests

A developer is often unsure of the validity of a test, whether it's because the production code has been phased out, the test or production code is too complex, or something is just plum broken. So each of the ScalaTest traits lets you temporarily disable certain tests. How a test is ignored depends on the trait, and the various ways will be covered with their respective traits.

To ignore any poor or broken test, replace the `it` keyword with `ignore`. The following example adds another test to the `FunSpec`. This test is ignored though, because it uses `ignore` instead of `it`.

```
package com.oreilly.testingscala

import org.scalatest.FunSpec
import org.scalatest.matchers.ShouldMatchers

class AlbumSpec extends FunSpec with ShouldMatchers {
  describe("An Album") {

    //Code removed for brevity

    ignore("can add a Producer to an album at construction time") {
      new Album("Breezin\'", 1976, new Artist("George", "Benson"))
      //TODO: Figure out the implementation of an album producer
    }
  }
}
```

In this example, which perhaps is oversimplified, the developer may be stalled while waiting for more information about the data set or the application. If you view the response from the SBT console or command prompt, the earlier tests are still valid and run, while the ignored test is displayed with a message stating that it has been ignored.

```
[info] AlbumSpec:
[info] An Album
[info] - can add an Artist to the album at construction time
[info] - can add a Producer to an album at construction time !!! IGNORED !!!
```

Simply changing `ignore` to `it` will make the test available for testing.

Tagging

Tagging categorizes tests so that they can run as part of a group. Tagging is very much like tagging a blog entry, where the subject of the blog entry is categorized with keywords so that not only can search engines find the entry, but users can click a word cloud to see similar entries. In testing, it is very useful to categorize tests for several reasons:

- Some tests are slow and you might want to skip them at times.
- Some tests check related functionality and should be run together.
- You may want to categorize tests as unit tests, integration tests, acceptance tests, or any other type.

While this book focuses mostly on unit testing using test-driven development there are other type of testing. *Integration testing* involves tests whose objects work with another, or examines how objects work with outside systems or the Internet. Integration testing takes place after unit testing, therefore after test-driven development.

Another level of testing is *acceptance testing*, which takes the program out for a test drive to see whether it is ready for deployment. Acceptance testing deals with usability and how the stakeholders of the product react to the developer's masterpiece.

Outside of these main levels of testing, there are other categories to consider. *Security testing*: how carefully contained and safe is the code? *Performance testing*: How fast does the application respond in production? *Load and stress testing*: In a server environment, how many users can hit the server, and can the server respond adequately?

Though it is difficult, many projects do have unit, integration, and acceptance testing for all code that is developed.

All testing traits in ScalaTest can be tagged with strings describing the test. Each testing trait has its own methodology to tag the test, but when the tagging is done, tests can be run either from the command prompt or SBT.

Running Tags From the Command Prompt

To specify which tests should be included when invoking ScalaTest using the Runner, add the -n option followed either by the name of the tag or by a list of names of tags surrounded by double quotes. To exclude any test by tag, use the -l option. Examples will appear in the sections covering each individual Spec.

Running Tags in SBT

SBT cannot currrently invoke the test task with tags, but tags can be used with the test-only task. To run a specific tag for a particular test class, append -- to the name of the class and apply either the -n or -l options. As with the command line, the option is followed by an individual tag name or by a list tag names in double quotes. Each spec has its own methodology of tagging and will be covered appropriately in each individual Spec.

The main reason the test task does not recognize tags is that SBT is still its infancy (ScalaTest and Specs2 are mere toddlers) and each of the built-in testing frameworks supported by SBT must support tagging. At the time of writing, ScalaTest and Specs2 have tagging ability, but ScalaCheck does not.

Specifications

FunSpec

The following FunSpec is a full example mixing in some Informer, GivenWhenThen, adding pending and ignore and a tag.

src/test/scala/com/oreilly/testingscala/AlbumSpecAll.scala.

```scala
package com.oreilly.testingscala

import org.scalatest.matchers.ShouldMatchers
import org.scalatest.{Tag, GivenWhenThen, FunSpec}


class AlbumSpecAll extends FunSpec with ShouldMatchers with GivenWhenThen {
  describe("An Album") {
    it("can add an Artist to the album at construction time", Tag("construc-
tion")) {
      given("The album Thriller by Michael Jackson")
      val album = new Album("Thriller", 1981, new Artist("Michael", "Jackson"))

      when("the artist of the album is obtained")
```

```
        val artist = album.artist

        then("the artist should be an instance of Artist")
        artist.isInstanceOf[Artist] should be(true)

        and("the artist's first name and last name should be Michael Jackson")
        artist.firstName should be("Michael")
        artist.lastName should be("Jackson")
          info("This is still pending, since there may be more to accomplish in
  this test")
        pending
      }

      ignore("can add a Producer to an album at construction time") {
        //TODO: Add some logic to add a producer.
      }
    }
  }
```

The above is a complete test that contains most of the features in a regular FunSpec. The first test is tagged as a construction test. The first test also mixes in GivenWhenThen informer methods to provide some testing structure. It also contains a regular Inform er, and is finally marked as pending. The second test is ignored. Following is the end result of this particular FunSpec.

```
> ~test-only com.oreilly.testingscala.AlbumSpecAll
[info] AlbumSpecAll:
[info] An Album
[info] - can add an Artist to the album at construction time (pending)
[info]    + Given The album Thriller by Michael Jackson
[info]    + When Artist of the album is obtained
[info]    + Then the Artist should be an instance of Artist
[info]    + And the artist's first name and last name should be Michael Jackson
[info]    + This is still pending, since there may be more to accomplish in this
test
[info] - can add a Producer to an album at construction time !!! IGNORED !!!
[info] Passed: : Total 2, Failed 0, Errors 0, Passed 0, Skipped 2
```

This is a sample of running a test, to only invoke tests with the tag of construction. Note that the ignored test of the FunSpec did not run since it wasn't tagged with the "construction" tag.

```
> ~test-only com.oreilly.testingscala.AlbumSpecAll -- -n construction
[info] AlbumSpecAll:
[info] An Album
[info] - can add an Artist to the album at construction time (pending)
[info]    + Given The album Thriller by Michael Jackson
[info]    + When Artist of the album is obtained
[info]    + Then the Artist should be an instance of Artist
```

```
[info]   + And the artist's first name and last name should be Michael Jackson
[info]   + This is still pending, since there may be more to accomplish in this
test
[info] Passed: : Total 1, Failed 0, Errors 0, Passed 0, Skipped 1
```

WordSpec

A WordSpec is another type of Spec available in ScalaTest. WordSpec makes heavy use
of the items when, should, and can with the ability to combine these words with any
means possible. when, should, and can are methods belonging to String by use of
implicit wrapper. Implicit wrappers are Scala's way of adding functionality to a class.
Let's continue on our musical journey, this time to the Hotel California.

```scala
package com.oreilly.testingscala

import org.scalatest.matchers.ShouldMatchers
import org.scalatest.WordSpec

class AlbumWordSpec extends WordSpec with ShouldMatchers {
  "An Album" when {
    "created" should {
      "accept the title, the year, and a Band as a parameter, and be able to
read
        those parameters back" in {
        new Album("Hotel California", 1977,
          new Band("The Eagles", new Artist("Don", "Henley"),
            new Artist("Glenn", "Frey"),
            new Artist("Joe", "Walsh"),
            new Artist("Randy", "Meisner"),
            new Artist("Don", "Felder")))
      }
    }
  }
}
```

Of course, the existing code must have some changes to make this new test work. First
off, an Act class is created. Act will be a superclass for both an Artist and a new class,
Band. Album will be refactored to include multiple acts instead of just one artist. Ar
tist will also be refactored to extend an Act.

src/main/scala/com/oreilly/testingscala/Act.scala.

```scala
package com.oreilly.testingscala

class Act
```

src/main/scala/com/oreilly/testingscala/Album.scala.

```scala
package com.oreilly.testingscala

class Album (val title:String, val year:Int, val acts:List[Act])
```

src/main/scala/com/oreilly/testingscala/Band.scala.

```
package com.oreilly.testingscala

class Band(name:String, members:List[Artist]) extends Act
```

WordSpec also gives the developer a different perspective on testing by forcing him to consider many when cases. In the AlbumWordSpec example, conditions are defined before any assertions. Each specification is a sentence in its own right. With the when we declare the subject of the test, followed by a block. The should block can be used with a subject or a condition of the test. For example, we can create another test that declares the subject within a should clause.

src/main/scala/com/oreilly/testingscala/AlbumWordSpec.scala.

```
"An album" should {
  "throw an IllegalArgumentException if there are no acts when created" in {
    intercept[IllegalArgumentException] {
      new Album("The Joy of Listening to Nothing", 1980, List())
    }
  }
}
```

The last example introduces some new concepts. The intercept[IllegalArgumentEx ception] is a method that takes a type parameter and has a block that will trap an exception defined in the type parameter of intercept, in this case, an IllegalArgumen tException. If an IllegalArgumentException is not caught within the intercept block the test will fail, stating that the Exception that was expected was not thrown.

Another concept from the last example that may be unfamiliar is List(): _*. This has nothing to do with ScalaTest: it is a Scala workaround that converts any scala.Seq to fit into a varargs declaration. Since Album's third parameter in its main constructor, acts, is a vararg declaration that accepts one or more Acts we must use the _* construct.

Naturally, the IllegalArgumentException has not been handled. Inserting a Scala require method will prevent any bad data from being applied during object construction.

```
package com.oreilly.testingscala

class Album (val title:String, val year:Int, val acts:Act*) {
  require(acts.size > 0)
}
```

The last example uses informers to verify that the intercept successfully traps the Ille galArgumentException. We can continue to add more lines to the lines, possibly to add more assertions.

FeatureSpec

FeatureSpec is a test that categorizes a test in a set of features. A feature is simply a single feature of the software that is to be delivered. Each feature will have various scenarios of that feature. Each scenario represents a successful or failed test that defines what the object under the test can or cannot do. The more scenarios per feature, the less doubt remains that an object is unstable.

Each feature must have a unique string to describe the desired feature of the software that is being tested. Each scenario string must also be unique.

```
package com.oreilly.testingscala

import org.scalatest.matchers.ShouldMatchers
import org.scalatest.FeatureSpec

class AlbumFeatureSpec extends FeatureSpec with ShouldMatchers {
    feature("An album's default constructor should support a parameter that ac-
cepts
        Option(List(Tracks)) ") { ... }
    feature("An album should have an addTrack method that takes a track and re-
turns
        an immutable copy of the Album with the added track") { ... }
}
```

In the above example, `AlbumFeatureSpec` of course will extend the `FeatureSpec` trait and the `ShouldMatchers` trait for the `should` assertion language. The example `FeatureSpec+` is divided up into features. These features are essentially a list of deliverables for the object that is under test.

In this example, an `Album` should have another constructor that handles an option of a list of new objects called `Tracks`. The final feature is that an `Album` should have a method called `addTrack` that accepts a new `Track` object and returns another immutable `Album` instance.

 Options in Scala are a near replacement for `null`. Instead of expressing no result in a return value as `null`, which was standard in Java and C++, a Scala developer would return `None`. If there is a value that can be returned it would be wrapped in `Some`. For example, returning the years the Cleveland Browns won the Super Bowl would return `None`, and for the San Francisco 49ers, a choice would be `Some(1981, 1984, 1988, 1989, 1994)`. Learning Scala is not in the scope of this book: please refer to *Programming Scala* for more information on the `Option[T]` type.

Implementing the first feature, we wish to create a couple of scenarios.

- An Album is given a list of 3 tracks exactly

- An Album is given an empty list

- An Album is given null

```
package com.oreilly.testingscala

import org.scalatest.matchers.ShouldMatchers
import org.scalatest.FeatureSpec

class AlbumFeatureSpec extends FeatureSpec with ShouldMatchers {
  feature("An album's default constructor should support a parameter that
      accepts Option(List(Tracks))") {
    scenario ("Album's default constructor is given a list of the 3 tracks
        exactly for the tracks parameter") {pending}
    scenario ("Album's default constructor is given an empty List for the
        tracks parameter") {pending}
    scenario ("Album's default constructor is given null for the tracks
        parameter") {pending}
  }
  feature("An album should have an addTrack method that takes a track and re-
turns an immutable copy of the Album with the added track") {  }
}
```

These examples are drawn out to reenact how test-driven development would look as
you're working with ScalaTest. They also show how pending can be used just to hold a
space for the developer to fill in the test later. AlbumFeatureSpec in the above example
is intended to add a few scenarios and list them as pending. The next phase will be to
start implementing some of these tests.

src/test/scala/com/oreilly/testingscala/AlbumFeatureSpec.scala.

```
package com.oreilly.testingscala

import org.scalatest.matchers.ShouldMatchers
import org.scalatest.FeatureSpec

class AlbumFeatureSpec extends FeatureSpec with ShouldMatchers {
  feature("An album's default constructor should support a parameter that ac-
cepts
      Option(List(Tracks))") {
    scenario("Album's default constructor is given a list of the 3 tracks exact-
ly
        for the tracks parameter") {
      val depecheModeCirca1990 = new Band("Depeche Mode",
        new Artist("Dave", "Gahan"),
        new Artist("Martin", "Gore"),
        new Artist("Andrew", "Fletcher"),
        new Artist("Alan", "Wilder"))

      val blackCelebration = new Album("Black Celebration", 1990,
```

```
        List(new Track("Black Celebration"),
          new Track("Fly on the Windscreen"),
          new Track("A Question of Lust")), depecheModeCirca1990: _*)

      album.tracks should have size(3)
    }

    scenario("Album's default constructor is given an empty List for the
        tracks parameter") {pending}
    scenario("Album's default constructor is given null for the tracks
        parameter") {pending}
  }
  feature("An album should have an addTrack method that takes a track and
      returns an immutable copy of the Album with the added track") {pending}
}
```

The first scenario is filled in the previous example. The test creates a band
depecheModeCirca1990+, and attempts to create an album, blackCelebration, with a
list of Tracks. This moment is a good time to look back and judge the API—is it clear
and understandable? Is it a clean API?

At this time, you may want to create some feature or scenario with pending after
thinking through the design of the Album object—before the brain becomes occupied
with other thoughts.

After the design introspection, and jotting down some ideas with feature and scenar
io, create the Track class (just enough to satisfy the test—no more, no less), and modify
the parameters of the Album constructor to satisfy the test and make it pass.

/src/main/scala/com/oreilly/testingscala/Album.scala.

```
class Album (val title:String, val year:Int, val tracks:Option[List[Track]],
val acts:Act*) {

    require(acts.size > 0)

      def this(title:String, year:Int, acts:Act*) = this (title, year, None,
acts:_*)
}
```

/src/main/scala/com/oreilly/testingscala/Track.scala.

```
package com.oreilly.testingscala

class Track(name:String)
```

The constructor for Album has been updated to include the parameter for track with a
type of Option[List[Track]]. The acts parameter has been moved to the last parameter, since according to the Scala specification, any repeated parameter must be the last
of a function or method. In the last example, the Track class was created.

The next example is the implementation for the next scenario: "Album's default constructor is given an empty List for the tracks parameter." This time, though, it will use the GivenWhenThen trait to structure the test.

```
package com.oreilly.testingscala

import org.scalatest.matchers.ShouldMatchers
import org.scalatest.{GivenWhenThen, FeatureSpec}

class AlbumFeatureSpec extends FeatureSpec with ShouldMatchers with GivenWhenThen {
    feature("An album's default constructor should support a parameter that accepts
        Option(List(Tracks))") {

    //Lines removed for brevity

    scenario("Album's default constructor is given a None for the tracks
        parameter") {
      given("the band, the Doobie Brothers from 1973")
      val theDoobieBrothersCirca1973 = new Band("The Doobie Brothers",
          new Artist("Tom", "Johnston"),
        new Artist("Patrick", "Simmons"),
        new Artist("Tiran", "Porter"),
        new Artist("Keith", "Knudsen"),
        new Artist("John", "Hartman"))


      when("the album is instantiated with the title, the year, none tracks,
          and the Doobie Brothers")
      val album = new Album("The Captain and Me", 1973, None,
          theDoobieBrothersCirca1973)

      then("calling the albums's title, year, tracks, acts property should yield
          the same results")
      album.title should be("The Captain and Me")
      album.year should be(1973)
      album.tracks should be(None)
      album.acts(0) should be(theDoobieBrothersCirca1973)
    }

    //Lines removed for brevity
  }
}
```

In the above example, what gets generated in the output in SBT is a very fluid statement of how the test performed.

```
An album's default constructor should support a parameter that accepts
    Option(List(Tracks))
[info]   Scenario: Album's default constructor is given a list of the 3 tracks
    exactly for the tracks parameter
```

```
[info]    Scenario: Album's default constructor is given a None for the tracks
    parameter
[info]       Given the band, the Doobie Brothers from 1973
[info]       When the album is instantiated with the title, the year, none tracks,
    and the Doobie Brothers
[info]       Then calling the albums's title, year, tracks, acts property should
    yield the same results
```

FreeSpec

FreeSpec is a test that is free of any restraint; the developer can craft it however she sees fit. Each element is of the story line is a string followed by -{. FreeSpec is engineered for the testing developer who wishes not to adhere to any pre-fabricated structure. FreeSpec tests are also attractive for test-driven developers who don't use or prefer English as a primary testing language.

GivenWhenThen can be useful in FreeSpec just to bring some structure into the test if needed.

```scala
package com.oreilly.testingscala

import org.scalatest.matchers.ShouldMatchers
import org.scalatest.FreeSpec

class JukeboxFreeSpec extends FreeSpec with ShouldMatchers {

  "given 3 albums" - {
    val badmotorfinger = new Album("Badmotorfinger", 1991, None,
        new Band("Soundgarden"))
    val thaDoggFather = new Album("The Dogg Father", 1996, None,
        new Artist("Snoop Doggy", "Dogg"))
    val satchmoAtPasadena = new Album("Satchmo At Pasadena", 1951, None,
        new Artist("Louis", "Armstrong"))
    "when a juke box is instantiated it should accept some albums" -{
      val jukebox = new JukeBox(Some(List(badmotorfinger, thaDoggFather,
          satchmoAtPasadena)))
      "then a jukebox's album catalog size should be 3" in {
        jukebox.albums.get should have size (3)
      }
    }
  }

  "El constructor de Jukebox puedo aceptar la palabra clave de 'None'" - {
    val jukebox = new JukeBox(None)
    "y regresas 'None' cuando llamado" in {
      jukebox.albums should be(None)
    }
  }
}
```

In `FreeSpec`, the developer has free reign with the structure. Each statement that doesn't contain any tests within the block terminates with `-{`. If the statement will contain the assertions required for the test, then an `in` keyword is required. In the above example, within the `"given some albums"` block, three albums of varying genres are instantiated. Within the next block, `"when a juke box is intantiated it should accept some albums"` a Jukebox is instantiated with the `Some` list of `Albums`. Again, each of these statements end in `-{` since these blocks do not contain any of the assertions within. The block `then a jukebox's album catalog size should be 3` on the other hand does contain an assertion there that block ends with `in  {` instead of `-{`.

In the last block of `JukeboxFreeSpec` the test is written in Spanish, since a `FreeSpec` and with the exception of the keyword `in`. It doesn't force any rules like `should`, `when`, etc. in a test. To translate, the first statement of the second test says "The constructor of jukebox should accept the keyword *None*. The last statement of the second test says "and return *None* when called" after the test assertion is made.

Just to finish out this section, the production code resulting from these tests has changed. For readers who are keeping track, the following is what `JukeBox` could look like.

```
package com.oreilly.testingscala

class JukeBox (val albums:Option[List[Album]]) {
  def readyToPlay = albums.isDefined
}
```

FlatSpec

For the developer with simple tastes, there is the FlatSpec, a no-nonsense, flat behavior-driven design spec meant to just declare the purpose of the test and implement it. `FlatSpec` is so named since the test is flat and lined up against the left side of the test. `FlatSpec` can either be written in a long or short form. First, here is the long form.

```
package com.oreilly.testingscala

import org.scalatest.matchers.MustMatchers
import org.scalatest.FlatSpec
import org.joda.time.Period

class TrackFlatSpec extends FlatSpec with MustMatchers {
  behavior of "A Track"

  it should """have a constructor that accepts the name and the length of the
      track
              in min:sec and returns a joda.time.Period when track.period is
                  called""" in {
    val track = new Track("Last Dance", "5:00")
    track.period must be(new Period(0, 5, 0, 0))
  }
```

```
it must """throw an IllegalArgumentException with the message \"Track name
    cannot be blank\"
            if the name of the track is blank.""" in {
    val exception = evaluating(new Track("")) must produce
        [IllegalArgumentException]
    exception.getMessage must be ("requirement failed: Track name cannot be
        blank")
    }
}
```

The TrackFlatSpec example above extends the FlatSpec trait, and is using MustMatch
ers for must assertion grammar. In a FlatSpec the declaration of the class under a test
occurs first, followed by one or more sentence specifications.

In the above example, the subject is Track. Each sentence specification supports the
subject. Each supporting sentence specification starts with the word it followed by
should, must, or can. The use of should, must, or can has nothing to do with the
MustMatchers or ShouldMatchers trait. Those keywords belong to the FlatSpec trait.
Looking at the above example, the first sentence specification uses it should, while the
second sentence specification uses it must. At the end of each of sentence specification
the word it is used as it is in other ScalaTest traits—to encapsulate the test logic.

Given the above test example, the Track class has changes that need to be made in order
to satisfy the test.

```
package com.oreilly.testingscala

import org.joda.time.format.PeriodFormatterBuilder

class Track(val name: String, val length: String) {

  require(name.trim().length() != 0, "Track name cannot be blank")

  def this(name: String) = this (name, "0:00")

  def period = {
    val fmt = new PeriodFormatterBuilder()
      .printZeroAlways()
      .appendMinutes()
      .appendSeparator(":")
      .printZeroAlways()
      .appendSeconds()
      .toFormatter()
    fmt.parsePeriod(length)
  }
}
```

This implementation uses the idea of a Period in Joda Time. A Period is a period of
time that is not tied to any chronological calendar or any time zone. It specifies a length

of time without an exact start or end time, and without measuring milliseconds. This is perfect for mesauring and storing a music track's length of time. The above example also uses a `PeriodFormatterBuilder` to create a `Parser` and `Printer` of the `Period`. A `Parser` will convert a `String` representation like "05:00" to a 5-minute `Period`. A `Printer` will do the opposite and convert a `Period` object into a `String` represenation. `PeriodFormatterBuilder` uses a `Builder` design pattern. The `Builder` pattern typically starts with an object, and allows the developer to add certain ingredients into that builder to create a custom object. In the above example, `PeriodFormatterBuilder` is instantiated, and certain elements are added to create the perfect `Formatter` for our needs. For more information on `Period`, visit the Joda-Time website (*http://joda-time.sourceforge.net/ key_period.html*). For more information on the `Builder` design pattern, please refer to *Head First Design Patterns* by Eric Freeman, Elisabeth Robson, Bert Bates, and Kathy Sierra and published by O'Reilly.

JUnitSuite

For the developer who fancies classic testing structures. ScalaTest supports JUnit testing using a `JUnitSuite` trait. The test class must extend `JUnitTestSuite` to mark the test as a JUnit-style test. The rest is tried-and-true JUnit. To include JUnit in the project, modify the *build.sbt* file to include the repository location of the latest JUnit library. At the time of this writing, JUnit is at 4.10.

```
libraryDependencies ++= Seq("org.scalatest" % "scalatest_2.9.2" % "1.8" % "test"
    withSources() withJavadoc(),
                        "joda-time" % "joda-time" % "1.8" withSources()
                            withJavadoc(),
                        "junit" % "junit" % "4.10" withSources()
                            withJavadoc())
```

In the above snippet of the *build.sbt* file, `"junit" % "junit" % "4.10" withSources() withJavadoc())` is added to the `Seq` of repository vectors. After adding the dependencies required for JUnit, reload and update the project using `sbt`.

The following sample creates a mutable `artist` member variable that is used to hold the subject under test, in this case an `artist`. The subject under test undergoes two distinct tests using a distinct `artist` that is initialized with the `startup()` method.

```
package com.oreilly.testingscala

import org.scalatest.junit.JUnitSuite
import org.junit.{Test, Before}
import org.junit.Assert._

class ArtistJUnitSuite extends JUnitSuite {
  var artist:Artist = _

  @Before
```

```
def startUp() {
  artist = new Artist("Kenny", "Rogers")
}

@Test
def addOneAlbumAndGetCopy() {
  val copyArtist = artist.addAlbum(new Album("Love will turn you around",
      1982, artist))
  assertEquals(copyArtist.albums.size, 1)
}

@Test
def addTwoAlbumsAndGetCopy() {
  val copyArtist = artist
    .addAlbum(new Album("Love will turn you around", 1982, artist))
    .addAlbum(new Album("We've got tonight", 1983, artist))
  assertEquals(copyArtist.albums.size, 2)
}
}
```

For those unfamiliar with JUnit, it was the first open-source testing framework developed for Java. The original JUnit ran by creating methods that started with the word test. If the JUnit Test Runner encountered a method named testEquality and the method started with the word test, the method would be executed as a test. With the advent of Java 1.5, annotations became popular for Java developers and JUnit started using @Test annotations to let the JUnit Test Runner know that the method is a test. For developers who are feeling particularly nostalgic, there is a JUnit3Suite that can be used to relive the testing methodology from JUnit 3.x.

The @Before annotation is used to tell the runner that the startUp() method in our example is to run before each method of the test is run. Therefore for each test, a new instance of Kenny Rogers will be created before the test. This ensures that each test has a Kenny Rogers of its own. Truly, a benefit.

Not shown here, the @After annotation is used on method that preforms and cleanup after the test. The reason for a cleanup in the above example is there is no need to set the artist to Kenny Rogers again. If that were required, the following code would be used for the cleanup method.

```
@After
def shutDown() {this.artist = null}
```

The method shutDown() is a kind of hack since the JUnitSuite is not immutable. If you are thinking that making the call def shutDown() {this.artist = _} would've worked, it wouldn't—since within a block the _ is considered a parameter of the function that makes up the method, therefore setting it to null is required. An unfortunate circumstance, but such manipulation is sometimes required in order to make a Scala method with a Java method.

The `@Before` and `@After` constructs are known as fixtures. Fixtures provide the setup and `tearDown`/`shutDown` methods that are used. Up to this point, fixtures in ScalaTest have not been covered, but we will discuss these strategies later in this chapter.

TestNGSuite

TestNG is another popular Java-based testing framework, with many more features than JUnit. It brought many new ideas to the Java testing worlds, including `DataProviders` —which can provide a list of data to a testing method—and groups—which are analogous to tagging in ScalaTest. These are only a few of the features included in TestNG. ScalaTest takes great care to ensure that all the TestNG features work under ScalaTest. First, it's necessary to include `testng` in the `libraryDependencies` setting of `build.sbt`. Below is a snippet to include the a `testng` dependency in the Seq of dependency vectors.

```
libraryDependencies ++= Seq("org.scalatest" % "scalatest_2.9.2" % "1.8" % "test"
    withSources() withJavadoc(),
                        "joda-time" % "joda-time" % "1.8" withSources()
                            withJavadoc(),
                        "junit" % "junit" % "4.10" withSources()
                            withJavadoc(),
                        "org.testng" % "testng" % "6.1.1" % "test"
                            withSources() withJavadoc())
```

After completing the `reload` and `update` required to bring the `testng` dependency into the project, the following is a sample of a TestNG test used in ScalaTest using a `Data Provider` and TestNG groups.

```
package com.oreilly.testingscala

import org.scalatest.testng.TestNGSuite
import collection.mutable.ArrayBuilder
import org.testng.annotations.{Test, DataProvider}
import org.testng.Assert._

class ArtistTestNGSuite extends TestNGSuite {

  @DataProvider(name = "provider")
  def provideData = {
    val g = new ArrayBuilder.ofRef[Array[Object]]()
    g += (Array[Object]("Heart", 5.asInstanceOf[java.lang.Integer]))
    g += (Array[Object]("Jimmy Buffet", 12.asInstanceOf[java.lang.Integer]))
    g.result()
  }


  @Test(dataProvider = "provider")
```

```
    def testTheStringLength(n1:String, n2:java.lang.Integer) {
        assertEquals(n1.length, n2)
    }
}
```

`provideData` is a method that returns an `Array[Array[Object]]` with test data used for the test. `provideData` is also annotated with `@DataProvider` and given an arbitrary name: `provider`. The data provided by the provider will call a test method requesting the data using the `dateProvider` parameter in a `Test` annotation. In the same, `test TheStringLength` method is annotated with `Test` and requests the data provider named `provider`. The `testTheStringLength` will now become two tests—one for each row of data provided by the provider. This strategy cuts boilerplate code down, and gives the test developer and a single point of focus for testing.

Below are the results generated from `ArtistTestNGSuite`.

```
> ~test-only com.oreilly.testingscala.ArtistTestNGSuite
[TestNG] Running:
  Command line suite

\=================================================
Command line suite
Total tests run: 2, Failures: 0, Skips: 0
\=================================================

[info] ArtistTestNGSuite:
[info] ArtistTestNGSuite:
[info] - testTheStringLength(Heart,5)
[info] - testTheStringLength(Jimmy Buffet,12)
[info] Passed: : Total 2, Failed 0, Errors 0, Passed 2, Skipped 0
[success] Total time: 1 s, completed Dec 27, 2011 3:08:48 PM
```

Of course, what good is a test if you can't tag for filtering purposes? In TestNG, tagging is called groups, and groups can be leveraged along with ScalaTest to include the groups in a test and run as if they were tags. In the following example, the method `testTheStringLength` test annotation will also include the group tag `word_count_analysis`.

```
@Test(dataProvider = "provider", groups=Array("word_count_analysis"))
  def testTheStringLength(n1:String, n2:java.lang.Integer) {
      assertEquals(n1.length, n2)
  }
```

Running the test again in sbt, this time with the -n switch for test only to include tests with `word_count_analysis` will run the same results.

```
> ~test-only com.oreilly.testingscala.ArtistTestNGSuite -- -n word_count_analy-
sis
[TestNG] Running:
  Command line suite
```

```
\===============================================
Command line suite
Total tests run: 2, Failures: 0, Skips: 0
\===============================================

[info] ArtistTestNGSuite:
[info] ArtistTestNGSuite:
[info] - testTheStringLength(Heart,5)
[info] - testTheStringLength(Jimmy Buffet,12)
[info] Passed: : Total 2, Failed 0, Errors 0, Passed 2, Skipped 0
[success] Total time: 1 s, completed Dec 27, 2011 3:07:50 PM
```

Fixtures

Each test can potentially have the same subject or subjects under test. Each test also has
the potential of using the same object dependencies or data used in each test. It makes
no sense to constantly set up each of those subjects and their dependencies. A fixture is
the ability to create these subjects and their dependenies once and have them be reused
in each test. Fixtures can allow either the same instance or different dependencies based
on the needs of the test, and can also allow sharing of testing structures to ensure that
certain rules pass regardless of the object being used. The Scala language itself has
methods to do some of the "fixturing" for the developer, while ScalaTest contains some
solutions of its own. Each Spec also has its way of producing these fixtures. JUnit and
TestNG integration, which is covered in later sections, also contains its own fixture
structures.

Anonymous Objects

First fixture strategy doesn't require anything from ScalaTest, since the solution is purely
a Scala solution. It uses an anonymous object, which is just a fancy term for an object
that can be created without a name. The anonymous object, once created, can be reused
in every test, and it will generate a brand-new dependency object upon request.

```
package com.oreilly.testingscala

import org.scalatest.matchers.ShouldMatchers
import org.scalatest.FunSpec

class AlbumFixtureSpec extends FunSpec with ShouldMatchers {

  def fixture = new {
    val letterFromHome = new Album("Letter from Home", 1989,
        new Band("Pat Metheny Group"))
  }

  describe("The Letter From Home Album by Pat Metheny") {
    it("should get the year 1989 from the album") {
```

```
    val album = fixture.letterFromHome
    album.year should be (1989)
  }
 }
}
```

The above specification contains a `fixture` method that creates an anonymous object in Scala with the variable `letterFromHome`. Every time the method `fixture` is called, a new object is always created. This creates a unique fixture for each individual test. Within the test block, the call `fixture.letterFromHome` will provide a unique `Album`. If the `Album` in this case were mutable, any other tests within the `Spec` would not get the mutated object that was changed in another test.

Just to drive the point home even futher, instead of using an immutable object like `Album`, the following example will use a mutable collection: `AlbumMutableFixtureS pec` will use a ListBuffer, which is a mutable list of objects—in this case, a list of albums.

```
package com.oreilly.testingscala

import org.scalatest.FunSpec
import org.scalatest.matchers.ShouldMatchers

class AlbumMutableFixtureSpec extends FunSpec with ShouldMatchers {
  def fixture = new {
    import scala.collection.mutable._
    val beachBoys = new Band("Beach Boys")
    val beachBoysDiscography = new ListBuffer[Album]()
    beachBoysDiscography += (new Album("Surfin' Safari", 1962, beachBoys))
  }

  describe("Given a single fixture each beach boy discography initially
      contains a single album") {
    it("then after 1 album is added, the discography size should have 2") {
      val discographyDeBeachBoys = fixture.beachBoysDiscography
      discographyDeBeachBoys += (new Album("Surfin' Safari", 1962,
          fixture.beachBoys))
      discographyDeBeachBoys.size should be(2)
    }

    it("then after 2 albums are added, the discography size should return 3") {
      val discographyDeBeachBoys = fixture.beachBoysDiscography
      discographyDeBeachBoys += (new Album("Surfin' Safari", 1962,
          fixture.beachBoys))
      discographyDeBeachBoys += (new Album("All Summer Long", 1964,
          fixture.beachBoys))
      discographyDeBeachBoys.size should be(3)
    }
  }
}
```

Both tests in the above example will pass. The fixture is a factory that generates a very basic Beach Boys discography and each time `fixture.beachBoysDiscography` is called a new instance is passed. If instead only an instance of the discography, rather than a fixture, were used, then the discography would be shared and the instance used in one test would be the same used in another test. The results would vary and be inconsistent.

Fixture Traits

An alternate strategy with ScalaTest is to create a custom `Fixture` trait in order to ensure that each test gets a unique subject to test. Every trait that is mixed into an object retains it's own methods and is not shared. For a little catching up with Scala, a trait is much like an interface in Java, except that it is concrete and its member variables will be mixed into the class that extends the the trait. The following example is similar to the above test except that it employs a trait instead of an anonymous object.

```
package com.oreilly.testingscala

import org.scalatest.matchers.ShouldMatchers
import org.scalatest.FunSpec

class AlbumFixtureTraitSpec extends FunSpec with ShouldMatchers {

  trait AlbumFixture {
    val letterFromHome = new Album("Letter from Home", 1989,
        new Band("Pat Metheny Group"))
  }

  describe("The Letter From Home Album by Pat Metheny") {
    it("should get the year 1989 from the album") {
      new AlbumFixture {
        letterFromHome.year should be(1989)
      }
    }
  }
}
```

Using a trait for the fixture encapsulates all the fixtures required per test. In order to make use of the fixture, within each test, an anonymous instantiation of the `trait` is required. Above, `new AlbumFixture` is called to anonymously create an object that extends the `AlbumFixture` trait. Since the trait is mixed in, anything that extends the trait will have access to its variables, methods, and functions. Therefore, no special magic is required: `letterFromHome` is obtainable and ready to make assertions about its state.

OneInstancePerTest

Outside the strategies that come with the Scala language, ScalaTest has its strategy to guarantee that each test will have its very own instance. The next example uses a OneInstancePerTest trait to provide one instance per test.

```
package com.oreilly.testingscala

import org.scalatest.matchers.ShouldMatchers
import collection.mutable.ListBuffer
import org.scalatest.{FreeSpec, OneInstancePerTest}


class AlbumListOneInstancePerTestFreeSpec extends FreeSpec with ShouldMatchers
    with OneInstancePerTest {
  val graceJonesDiscography = new ListBuffer[Album]()
  graceJonesDiscography += (new Album("Portfolio", 1977, new Artist("Grace",
    "Jones")))

  "Given an initial Grace Jones Discography" - {
    "when an additional two albums are added, then the discography size should
        be 3" in {
      graceJonesDiscography += (new Album("Fame", 1978, new Artist("Grace",
        "Jones")))
      graceJonesDiscography += (new Album("Muse", 1979, new Artist("Grace",
        "Jones")))
      graceJonesDiscography.size should be(3)
    }

    "when one additional album is added, then the discography size
        should be 2" in {
      graceJonesDiscography += (new Album("Warm Leatherette", 1980,
        new Artist("Grace", "Jones")))
      graceJonesDiscography.size should be(2)
    }
  }

  "Given an initial Grace Jones Discography " - {
    "when one additional album from 1980 is added, then the discography size
should be 2" in {
        graceJonesDiscography += (new Album("Nightclubbing", 1981, new Ar-
tist("Grace", "Jones")))
      graceJonesDiscography.size should be(2)
    }
  }
}
```

The above example uses a subject that is a mutable ListBuffer of Album. Each grace Jones discography is generated per test. Since this test does indeed function and passes, the assertions prove that each test is getting its own discography. The special secret in this test is the `OneInstancePerTest` which will create a test suite per test. Therefore each test will have its own subjects and dependencies. The example uses a `FreeSpec` test. Each `Spec` in ScalaTest is different, and what is defined as a test in each spec is different. For the last example, a test is considered to be what is contained in the `in` clause of a test.

Before and After

To have the best control of what gets initialized as well as what gets torn down with a test, the trait `BeforeAndAfter` is the elixir to provide such functionality. In the following example, the `BeforeAndAfter` trait is included, this time with a `WordSpec` to initialize the Human League's discography with one album. During the test, another album is added, and an assertion is made on the size of the mutable discography. After the test, the mutable discography is cleared.

```
package com.oreilly.testingscala

import collection.mutable.ListBuffer
import org.scalatest.{BeforeAndAfter, WordSpec}
import org.scalatest.matchers.ShouldMatchers

class AlbumBeforeAndAfterFixtureSpec extends WordSpec with ShouldMatchers
    with BeforeAndAfter {
  val humanLeagueDiscography = new ListBuffer[Album]()

  before {
    info("Starting to populate the discography")
    humanLeagueDiscography += (new Album("Dare", 1981,
        new Band("Human League")))
  }

  "A mutable ListBuffer of albums" should {
    "have a size of 3 when two more albums are added to the Human League
        Discography" in {
      humanLeagueDiscography += (new Album("Hysteria", 1984,
          new Band("Human League")))
      humanLeagueDiscography += (new Album("Crash", 1986,
          new Band("Human League")))
      humanLeagueDiscography should have size (3)
    }

    "have a size of 2 when one more album is added to the Human League
        Discography" in {
      humanLeagueDiscography += (new Album("Romantic", 1990,
          new Band("Human League")))
      humanLeagueDiscography should have size (2)
    }
  }

  after {
```

```
        info("Clearing the discography")
        humanLeagueDiscography.clear()
    }
}
```

Some additional notes regarding the above example—first, the `before` and `after` blocks are members of the `BeforeAndAfter` trait. The trait also guarantees that the member variables of the `Spec`, in this case a `WordSpec`, are unique per each test. In a `WordSpec` the test is also defined by the `in` block. When running the example, notice the number of times a discography is initialized and also torn down. There are two because, like the `OneInstancePerTest`, a separate suite is created and used per test; therefore, there will always be more than one `before` and `after` invocation.

```
2. Waiting for source changes... (press enter to interrupt)
[info] Compiling 1 Scala source to /home/danno/testing_scala_book.git
    /testingscala/target/scala-2.9.2/test-classes...
[info] AlbumBeforeAndAfterFixtureSpec:
[info] A mutable ListBuffer of albums
[info] + Starting to populate the discography
[info] - should have a size of 3 when two more albums are added to
    the Human Discography
[info] + Clearing the discography
[info] + Starting to populate the discography
[info] - should have a size of 2 when one more album is added to
    the Human Discography
[info] + Clearing the discography
[info] Passed: : Total 2, Failed 0, Errors 0, Passed 2, Skipped 0
```

ScalaTest is an excellent testing framework. A study of the internals of the framework is also a great way to understand Scala, and to understand the language itself. ScalaTest's matching language is intuitive, and the different specification allows the test-driven developer to choose his own testing style. ScalaTest's integration with JUnit and TestNG is also valuable for the developer who wishes to bring tests from Java into Scala, making it a great entry point from Java to Scala. There is more to learn about ScalaTest and that is the integration with ScalaCheck as we will see in the last chapter of the book.

CHAPTER 4

Specs2

Specs2 (*http://etorreborre.github.com/specs2/*) is a testing framework with a different focus and perspective that's different from ScalaTest's. Much like ScalaTest's, Specs2 works with SBT, but it has some unique differences that a developer may choose based on the functionality needed. Specs2 has a different set of matchers, a different way of structuring tests, as well as DataTable specifications, AutoExamples, and Fitnesse style specifications used for collaboration purposes with the stakeholders of your project. Specs2 tests are also unique in that they are concurrently executed in each thread.

Setting Up Specs2 in SBT

Since the book is focused on testing frameworks used with SBT, the following setup in *build.sbt* will bring in some dependencies and resolvers that are required for Specs2 to run.

```
name := "Testing Scala"

version := "1.0"

scalaVersion := "2.9.2"

resolvers ++= Seq(
  "snapshots" at "http://scala-tools.org/repo-snapshots",
  "releases"  at "http://scala-tools.org/repo-releases")

resolvers ++= Seq(
  "sonatype-snapshots" at "http://oss.sonatype.org/content
      /repositories/snapshots",
  "sonatype-releases"  at "http://oss.sonatype.org/content
      /repositories/releases")

libraryDependencies ++= Seq(
  "org.scalatest" % "scalatest_2.9.2" % "1.8" % "test" withSources()
```

```
      withJavadoc(),
    "joda-time" % "joda-time" % "1.6.2" withSources() withJavadoc(),
    "junit" % "junit" % "4.10" withSources() withJavadoc(),
    "org.testng" % "testng" % "6.1.1" % "test" withSources() withJavadoc(),
    "org.specs2" %% "specs2" % "1.12.3" withSources() withJavadoc(),
```

The *build.sbt* file must be edited to include a new element: a `resolvers` setting. `resolvers` is a list or `Seq` of Maven repositories for SBT to look for any required dependencies. The `++=` operator is an SBT-0 overloaded operator that tells SBT to add the resolvers that follow the list that comes with SBT out of the box. The Specs2 library is housed in the `oss sonatype` repository, therefore the repository URLs must be declared so that sbt will know where to look. For Specs2, the `oss.sonatype.org` snapshot and release repository are required for the build so those URLs are added.

The first few elements in the `libraryDependencies` setting have already been described and used in the previous chapters. The last dependency is needed to use Specs2. The `specs2` dependency is the core library and as mentioned in the first chapter, `withSources()` and `withJavadoc()` will also download jar files containing the source code and the java/scaladoc respectively in the ivy local repository.

After making these amendments to `build.sbt`, run `sbt` and enter `reload` in the interactive shell, or run `sbt reload` at the shell command prompt.

Unit Specification

The first flavor of test in Specs2 is the unit specification. It has a similar intent to Scala-Test, but is distinguished by its structure and design.

```
package com.oreilly.testingscala

import org.specs2.mutable._
import org.joda.time.Period

class JukeboxUnitSpec extends Specification {
  "A Jukebox" should {
    """have a play method that returns a copy of the jukebox that selects
       the first song on the first album as the current track""" in {
      val groupTherapy = new Album("Group Therapy", 2011,
        Some(List(new Track("Filmic", "3:49"),
          new Track("Alchemy", "5:17"),
          new Track("Sun &amp; Moon", "5:25"),
          new Track("You Got to Go", "5:34"))), new Band("Above and Beyond"))
      val jukebox = new JukeBox(Some(List(groupTherapy)))
      val jukeboxNext = jukebox.play
      jukeboxNext.currentTrack.get.name must be_==("Filmic")
      jukeboxNext.currentTrack.get.period must be_==(new Period(0, 3, 49, 0))
```

```
        //Must be 3 minutes and 49 seconds
    }
  }
}
```

The unit specification in Spec2 starts with a string that describes the class undergoing the test. The description ends with a should method, and starts a block that should be familiar ground. Within the should block are one or more String test descriptions. The should block then ends with an in block containing the actual test code. In the previous example, "A Jukebox" specifies what is to be tested, and within the should block is one test, which describes a play method and the behavior that is expected from the test.

Note that this unit specification imports import org.specs2.mutable._. This is a different package from the acceptance specification covered later in this chapter.

The code within the in block contains a declaration of an album by the group Above and Beyond. The code also instantiates a jukebox with one album, runs the method play (which has not been implemented yet since we are TDDers). A jukebox is immutable, so invoking the method can't change the current state of the jukebox. Instead, it instantiates a new object and returns it with a different state. That new jukebox is assigned to the variable jukeboxNext. The last two lines of the test are the expectations. The test asserts that the current track name after play has been invoked is "Filmic" and that the Period of the track is 3 minutes and 49 seconds.

When comparing and contrasting Spec2 with ScalaTest, it should strike you that the matchers are different. In JukeboxUnitSpec, the test for equality uses must be_== instead of ScalaTest's must be (...). Each testing framework has its own set of matchers and its own strengths. In Spec2, each block of testing expectations returns a Result object.

Another interesting point is that all Specs2 tests are asynchronous and each runs in its thread using a Promise. Promises are processes that run on separate threads asynchronously using Actors and send objects, in this case an ExecutedResult to one another. Every Specs2 test sends each test as a message to an actor, and the result of the test is sent back as a ExecutedResult message.

In the previous test, the two expectations will generate a Result type of success. If any of the test expectations were to fail, a FailureException would be thrown, which encapsulates a Failure object. Contrast this with ScalaTest, which throws a Test FailedException if a test has failed. Specs2 offers a few more states to return for a test, including anError to indicate that some unknown exception has occured, skipped if the tester wishes for the test to be skipped at this time, and pending if the test is still under construction. The decision whether a test is skipped or pending follows the same logic as it does in ScalaTest.

The resulting production code is driven by the test.

```
package com.oreilly.testingscala

class JukeBox private (val albums:Option[List[Album]],
    val currentTrack:Option[Track]) {
  def this(albums:Option[List[Album]]) = this(albums, None)
  def readyToPlay = albums.isDefined
  def play = new JukeBox(albums, Some(albums.get(0).tracks.get(0)))
}
```

Specs2 offers two major constructs for authoring tests: at this time we are only covering unit specification. Specs2 offers varying ways to organize your tests. But first, a quick introduction of Specs2 matchers is in order to get a better feel for the framework.

Matchers

Specs2 offers an abundance of matchers, sometimes offering aliases for the same matchers just to offer the test developer a choice.

Simple Matchers

The following example tests for equality using Specs2 Matchers, showing how it differs from ScalaTest. The example uses Fleetwood Mac's *Rumours* album and merely tests the title. The second half of the example asserts that the title of the *Rumours* album has nothing to do with Aerosmith's *Sweet Emotion*.

```
val rumours= new Album("Rumours", 1977,
Some(List(new Track("Second Hand News", "2:43"),
    new Track("Dreams", "4:14"),
    new Track("Never Going Back Again", "2:02"),
    new Track("Don't Stop", "3:11"))), new Band("Fleetwood Mac"))

rumours.title must be_==("Rumours")
rumours.title must beEqualTo("Rumours")
rumours.title must_== ("Rumours")
rumours.title mustEqual "Rumours"
rumours.title should_== "Rumours"
rumours.title === "Rumours"
rumours.title must be equalTo ("Rumours")

rumours.title must not be equalTo("Sweet Emotion")
rumours.title must_!= "Sweet Emotion"
rumours.title mustNotEqual "Sweet Emotion"
rumours.title must be_!=("Sweet Emotion")
rumours.title !== "Sweet Emotion"
```

String Matchers

Specs2 also offers an extensive list of matchers meant specifically for strings, including some powerful regular expresssion matchers.

```
val boston = new Album("Boston", 1976,
  Some(List(new Track("More Than a Feeling", "4:44"),
    new Track("Peace of Mind", "5:02"),
    new Track("Foreplay/Long Time", "7:47"),
    new Track("Rock and Roll Band", "2:59"))), new Band("Boston"))

boston.title must beEqualTo("BoSTon").ignoreCase
boston.title must beEqualTo(" Boston").ignoreSpace
boston.title must beEqualTo(" BoStOn  ").ignoreSpace.ignoreCase
boston.title must contain ("os")
boston.title must startWith ("Bos")
boston.title must endWith ("ton")
boston.title must not startWith ("Char")
boston.title must have size(6)
boston.title must beMatching ("B\\w{4}n")
boston.title must beMatching ("""B\w{4}n""")
boston.title must =~("""B\w{4}n""")
boston.title must find("""(os.)""").withGroups("ost")
```

Most lines are self-explanatory. String can be matched with a must beMatching(...) method. The examples given use both the regular strings and raw strings, so there is no need to escape the backslash. beMatching can be replaced with =~. Finally, Specs2 string matching can find a substring with in a string and assert that the regular expression groups found are equal to the expected results. The regular expression B\w{4}n refers to a B followed by any four characters found in a word, and finishing with n.

Relational Operator Matchers

The following example reproduces the ScalaTest answer-of-life example from Relatio nalOperatorMatchers in ScalaTest to illustrate its relational operators. These operators can use either a DSL-like syntax or symbolic operators to set expectations.

```
val answerToLife = 42
answerToLife should be_<(50)
answerToLife should not be_>(50)
answerToLife must beLessThan(50)
answerToLife should be_>(3)
answerToLife must beGreaterThan(3)
answerToLife should be_<=(100)
answerToLife must beLessThanOrEqualTo(100)
answerToLife should be_>=(0)
answerToLife must beGreaterThanOrEqualTo(0)
answerToLife === (42)
```

Floating-Point Matchers

Specs2 also offers inexact measurements of floating-point calculations much like Scala-Test, but with a different DSL structure.

```
(4.0 + 1.2) must be_==(5.2)
(0.9 - 0.8) must beCloseTo (0.1, .01)
(0.4 + 0.1) must not beCloseTo (40.00, .30)
(0.4 + 0.1) must not be closeTo (40.00, .30)
```

Reference Matchers

Garth Brooks time again—this time analyzing reference matchers in Specs2.

```
val garthBrooks = new Artist("Garth", "Brooks")
val chrisGaines = garthBrooks

garthBrooks must beTheSameAs(chrisGaines)

val debbieHarry = new Artist("Debbie", "Harry")
garthBrooks must not beTheSameAs (debbieHarry)
```

Iterable Matchers

These use the same iterator tests from ScalaTest, with a few interesting new versions.

```
(Nil must be).empty
List(1, 2, 3) must not be empty
List(1, 2, 3) must contain(3)
List(1, 2, 3) must not contain (5)
List(4, 5, 6) must not contain(7, 8, 9)
List(1, 2, 3, 4, 5, 6) must contain(3, 4, 5).inOrder
List(4, 5, 6) must contain(4, 5, 6).only.inOrder
List(1, 2) must have size (2)
List(1, 2) must have length (2)
```

Seq and Traversable Matchers

Specs2 contains a some really neat tricks for asserting conditions within any Seq or Traversable.

```
List("Hello", "World") must containMatch("ll") // matches with .*ll.*
List("Hello", "World") must containMatch("Hello") // matches with .*ll.*
List("Hello", "World") must containPattern(".*llo") // matches with .*llo
List("Hello", "World") must containPattern("\\w{5}")
List("Hello", "World") must containMatch("ll").onlyOnce
List("Hello", "World") must have(_.size >= 5)
List("Hello", "World") must haveTheSameElementsAs(List("World", "Hello"))
```

The first and second lines determine whether any of the elements contain the string. The third and fourth lines determine whether any of the line items contain a particular pattern (regular expression). The fifth line calls a modifier method onlyOne, which asserts that ll is in a string of lists somewhere and that it occurs in that particular list only one time. The sixth matcher accepts a Boolean function and asserts that every element in the Traversable abides by it. In this case, each element must have a size greater than 5. The last line item matches the Seq on the left side with the Seq on the right side.

Map Matchers

Using the map of singers to bands shown in MapMatchers of ScalaTest, here are the analogous matchers for Specs2.

```
val map = Map("Jimmy Page" -> "Led Zeppelin", "Sting" -> "The Police",
    "Aimee Mann" -> "Til\' Tuesday")
map must haveKey("Sting")
map must haveValue("Led Zeppelin")
map must not haveKey ("Brian May")
map must havePair("Aimee Mann" -> "Til\' Tuesday")
```

All these methods are fairly straightforward. All matchers can determine whether the map has a particular key, a particular value, or pair. And each matcher can check the opposite expectations with a not modifier.

XML Matchers

Specs2 has some special sugar to determine whether two XML Elem elements are equal without regard to white space. For those still unfamiliar with Scala, Scala has built-in support for XML. Each XML element, is of type Elem; therefore, Specs2 can compare these objects and their spacing either strictly or leniently. Consider the sample ColdPlay album list that follows, where the <albums> parent tag nest five separate albums.

```
val coldPlayAlbums = <albums>
        <album name="Parachutes"/>
        <album name="A Rush of Blood to the Head"/>
        <album name="X&amp;Y"/>
        <album name="Viva la Vida or Death and All His Friends"/>
        <album name="Mylo Xyloto"/>
    </albums>
```

We might naively try to match it as follows, but the match will fail.

```
coldPlayAlbums must beEqualTo(<albums>
        <album name="Parachutes"/>
            <album name="A Rush of Blood to the Head"/>
        <album name="X&amp;Y"/>
        <album name="Viva la Vida or Death and All His Friends"/>
        <album name="Mylo Xyloto"/>
    </albums>)
```

The stack trace of the failed test is too hideous to paste in the book, but it shows that the match does not work even though both XML elements are equal, because beEqual To is tripped up by the different spacing. To test for XML equality, replace beEqualTo with beEqualToIgnoringSpace, or change be_== to be_==\.

```
coldPlayAlbums must beEqualToIgnoringSpace(<albums>
        <album name="Parachutes"/>
        <album name="A Rush of Blood to the Head"/>
      <album name="X&amp;Y"/>
      <album name="Viva la Vida or Death and All His Friends"/>
        <album name="Mylo Xyloto"/>
    </albums>)
```

Partial Function Matchers

Partial functions determine whether a predicate applies to their input and, if so, run the code you specify. The following example uses PartialFunctions to determine whether a given record is a gold album, a platinum album, or, as a joke, an alternative album.

```
val goldPartialFunction: PartialFunction[Int, String] = new PartialFunc-
tion[Int, String] {
  //States that this partial function will take on the task
  def isDefinedAt(x: Int) = x >= 500000

  //What we do if this does partial function matches
  def apply(v1: Int) = "Gold"
}

val platinumPartialFunction: PartialFunction[Int, String] = {case x: Int if
    (x >= 1000000) => "Platinum"}
val junkPartialFunction: PartialFunction[Int, String] = {case x: Int if
    (x < 500000) => "Alternative"}

val riaaCertification = goldPartialFunction
    orElse platinumPartialFunction orElse junkPartialFunction
riaaCertification must beDefinedAt (100)
riaaCertification must beDefinedBy (100 -> "Alternative")
```

GoldPartialFunction determines whether the number given is greater than 500,000 and, if so, returns Gold. platinumPartialFunction and junkPartialFunction are also partial functions, but are created through case statements. The variable riaaCertifi cation combines the three partial functions into one. riaaCertification accepts an Int input to represent the number of albums sold and outputs the resulting record status.

The line riaaCertification must beDefinedAt (100) asserts that the given value is supported in the riaaCertification partial function chain. The last line asserts that the given value to a partial function will indeed return the ideal result. This example asserts that, given album sales of 100, the result will be labeled as Alternative.

Other Matchers

A few more matchers come with the Specs2 matchers, and it's amazing that both Specs2 and ScalaTest push the envelope of matchers.

On a side note, Specs2 is very flexible when it comes to matchers, and you can make custom matchers if desired. In the following snippet of code, two matchers are created and can be used with in Specs2. beEven can be in an expectation that states 4 must beEven. "Flash" must beCapitalizedAs ("FLASH") The ^^ in the following code represents a function that returns what the expected value should be if an exception is returned. What is interesting about the last matcher is that it is built upon another Matcher, capitalized.

```
def beEven: Matcher[Int] = (i: Int) => (i % 2 == 0, i+" is even", i+" is odd")

def beCapitalizedAs(capitalized: String) = be_==(capitalized) ^^
    ((_:String).toUpperCase)
```

Acceptance Specification

An acceptance specification separates what the test is expected to do from what actually happens during the test. An oversimplified example of using a Specs2 acceptance specification follows.

```
package com.oreilly.testingscala

import org.specs2.Specification

class SimpleAcceptanceSpec extends Specification { def is =
  "This is a simple specification"        ^
      "and this should run f1"           ! f1 ^
      "and this example should run f2"   ! f2

  def f1 = success
  def f2 = pending
}
```

A very important item to note is the Specification that is imported into the package. This is org.specs2.Specification and not import org.specs2.mutable._, which is used in the unit specification that is covered in the first section of this chapter.

In SimpleAcceptanceSpec, the method that bootstraps the entire test for the class is the method is. The method returns a Fragments object containing all the examples. The SimpleAcceptanceSpec contains two examples. One will run the f1 method, as dictated after the intro string, and the next should run f2. The ! notation is used to divide the test and does so in its own separate thread.

Carets divide the specifications. Any string that does not call a method using the ! operator is considered a header for the following tests. For SimpleAcceptanceSpec, This is a simple specification is a string followed by a ^ but not a !, so it will not be considered a test and will merely echo the results of sbt or the Specs2 runner. On the other lines, the carets divide the specifications. The last line requires no final caret since it needs no division from a following specification.

The result from each of the actors are returned and the results are reported in SBT.

```
[info] Compiling 1 Scala source to /home/danno/testing_scala_book.git
    /testingscala/target/scala-2.9.2/test-classes...
[info] This is a simple specification
[info] + and this should run f1
[info] * and this example should run f2 PENDING
[info]
[info] Total for specification SimpleAcceptanceSpec
[info] Finished in 87 ms
[info] 2 examples, 0 failure, 0 error, 1 pending (+1)
[info] Passed: : Total 2, Failed 0, Errors 0, Passed 1, Skipped 1
[success] Total time: 5 s, completed Dec 28, 2011 9:22:26 PM
```

If you do not wish to run each method in its own thread, it can be annotated with an argument to make it sequential. To do this, merely add args(sequential=true) to the test as follows:

/src/test/scala/com/oreilly/testingscala/SimpleSequentialAcceptanceSpec.scala.

```
class SimpleSequentialAcceptanceSpec extends Specification { def is =
    args(sequential = true)                    ^
    "This is a simple specification"           ^
       "and this should run f1"            ! f1 ^
       "and this example should run f2"    ! f2

    def f1 = success
    def f2 = pending
}
```

In the specification results above, the + indicates that and this should run f1 ran successfully. The last test result shown next to PENDING and bears a * symbol to state that the test is pending. Notice that This is a simple specification has no preceding symbol, because the line never invoked an actor with !. It is just considered informational, much like the way informers are used in ScalaTest.

The previous example was boring, so it's time to get back to the music. We'll create a simple Artist test that adds a middle name to an artist and expects a fullName method to get the full name of the artist. The overall goal is to make sure that an Artist object can optionally include a middle name.

```
package com.oreilly.testingscala
```

```
import org.specs2.Specification

class ArtistAcceptanceSpec extends Specification { def is =
  "An artist should have a middle name at construction"                           ^
    """An artist should be able to be constructed with a middle name and
       get it back calling 'middleName'""" ! makeAnArtistWithMiddleName           ^
    """An artist should be able to have a full name made of the first
       and last name
       given a first and last name at construction time""" !
         testFullNameWithFirstAndLast                                             ^
    """An artist should be able to have a full name made of the first,
       middle and last name
         given a first, middle, and last name at construction time""" !
           testFullNameWithFirstMiddleAndLast


  def makeAnArtistWithMiddleName = pending
  def testFullNameWithFirstAndLast = pending
  def testFullNameWithFirstMiddleAndLast = pending
}
```

This is a beefier example of the test created initially in this section. Three test specifications support this topic. Each calls one of the three methods implemented in the following code and tests the results. All three testing results at the moment will return a Result of pending, because we're still thinking over how to implement the production code.

```
[info] Compiling 1 Scala source to /home/danno/testing_scala_book.git/testings-
cala
      /target/scala-2.9.2/test-classes...
[info] An artist should have a middle name at construction
[info] * An artist should be able to be constructed with a middle name and
[info]          get it back calling 'middleName' PENDING
[info] * An artist should be able to have a full name made of the first and
      last name
[info]          given a first and last name at construction time PENDING
[info] * An artist should be able to have a full name made of the first, middle
and last name
[info]             given a first, middle, and last name at construction time
PENDING
[info]
[info] Total for specification ArtistAcceptanceSpec
[info] Finished in 124 ms
[info] 3 examples, 0 failure, 0 error, 3 pendings
[info] Passed: : Total 3, Failed 0, Errors 0, Passed 0, Skipped 3
[success] Total time: 6 s, completed Dec 28, 2011 10:04:01 PM
```

Next it's time to fill in the pending specifications, and give them some concrete tests.

```
package com.oreilly.testingscala

import org.specs2.Specification
```

```
class ArtistAcceptanceSpec extends Specification { def is =
  "An artist should have a middle name at construction"                  ^
    """An artist should be able to be constructed with a Option[String]
       middle name and
       get it back calling 'middleName'""" ! makeAnArtistWithMiddleName ^
    """An artist should be able to have a full name made of the first
       and last name
       given a first and last name at construction time"""
          ! testFullNameWithFirstAndLast                                 ^
    """An artist should be able to have a full name made of the first,
       middle and last name
         given a first, middle, and last name at construction time"""
            ! testFullNameWithFirstMiddleAndLast


  def makeAnArtistWithMiddleName = {
    val vaughn = new Artist("Stevie", "Ray", "Vaughn")
    vaughn.middleName must be_==(Some("Ray"))
  }

  def testFullNameWithFirstAndLast = {
    val luther = new Artist("Luther", "Vandross")
    luther.fullName must be_==("Luther Vandross")
  }

  def testFullNameWithFirstMiddleAndLast = {
    val bonJovi = new Artist("Jon", "Bon", "Jovi")
    bonJovi.fullName must be_==("Jon Bon Jovi")
  }
}
```

The example fills in some expectations regarding the middle names for an Artist using
the artists Stevie Ray Vaughn, guitarist extraordinare; Luther Vandross, voice extraordinaire; and Jon Bon Jovi, steel horse rider extraordinaire.

Adding compile-time errors and run-time exceptions to meet the specification requirements, including breaking some of the previous tests, makes the production code more
robust with some extra functionality.

```
package com.oreilly.testingscala

case class Artist(firstName: String, middleName: Option[String],
    lastName: String, albums: List[Album]) extends Act {
  def this(firstName: String, lastName: String) = this (firstName, None,
      lastName, Nil)

  def this(firstName: String, middleName: String, lastName: String) =
      this (firstName, Some(middleName), lastName, Nil)

  def getAlbums = albums

  def addAlbum(album: Album) = new Artist(firstName, middleName, lastName,
```

```
      album :: albums)

  def fullName = middleName match {
    case Some(x) => firstName + " " + x + " " + lastName
    case _ => firstName + " " + lastName
  }
}
```

The changes in Artist include an extra parameter in the default constructor, and an additional constructor to support some of the older tests that still need to create an artist with first and last name only. The last method is a fullName method that uses pattern matching to determine whether the artist has a middle name; if so, it returns the first, middle, and last names divided by spaces; if not, it returns the first and last names. The results in SBT or the Specs2 runner show the progress of TDD.

```
[info] Compiling 1 Scala source to /home/danno/testing_scala_book.git/testings-
cala/target/scala-2.9.2/test-classes...
[info] An artist should have a middle name at construction
[info] + An artist should be able to be constructed with a Option[String] mid-
dle name and
[info]          get it back calling 'middleName'
[info] + An artist should be able to have a full name made of the first and
last name
[info]          given a first and last name at construction time
[info] + An artist should be able to have a full name made of the first, middle
and last name
[info]          given a first, middle, and last name at construction time
[info]
[info] Total for specification ArtistAcceptanceSpec
[info] Finished in 236 ms
[info] 3 examples, 0 failure, 0 error
[info] Passed: : Total 3, Failed 0, Errors 0, Passed 3, Skipped 0
[success] Total time: 5 s, completed Dec 28, 2011 10:45:29 PM
```

Specs2 offers formatting tags to prettify the end results of the tests. Some formatting is implicit. Any text that directly follows another is indented under the preceding text. Thus, in the previous example, An artist should have a middle name at construc tion is followed by a ^ to delineate the end of the line. Since the next element following the ^ is also a String, it is indented and labeled with a + mark.

Adjacent specification examples (examples defined by both the string description and the call to the test) will have the same indentation level. Thus, in the ArtistAcceptan ceSpec, the two specification examples will have the same indentation level.

```
"""An artist should be able to be constructed with a Option[String] middle name
and
        get it back calling 'middleName'"""  !  makeAnArtistWithMiddle-
Name                        ^
"""An artist should be able to have a full name made of the first and last name
    given a first and last name at construction time"""  !  testFullNameWithFirst-
AndLast
```

If either the next string after the specification or the specification example is not to be indented, you can add a ^p tag after the previous caret. The ^p tag terminates the line with a carriage return and decrements the indentation by 1 for the next specification example or string. This is nearly analogous to the <p> tag in HTML/XHTML. In the next example, a ^p is added to separate the test, since the next test will focus on creating an alias, and it is a perfect place to add a paragraph delimiter.

```
package com.oreilly.testingscala

import org.specs2.Specification

class ArtistAcceptanceSpec extends Specification { def is =
            "An     artist     should     have     a     middle     name     at     construc-
tion"                                                          ^
        """"An artist should be able to be constructed with a Option[String] mid-
dle name and
              get it back calling 'middleName'"""  ! makeAnArtistWithMiddle-
Name                                      ^
        """"An artist should be able to have a full name made of the first and
last name
          given a first and last name at construction time"""  ! testFullNameWith-
FirstAndLast                  ^
        """"An artist should be able to have a full name made of the first, middle
and last name
            given a first, middle, and last name at construction time"""  ! test-
FullNameWithFirstMiddleAndLast ^


                    p^
              "An        artist       should       have       an
alias"                                                          ^
        """"method called withAlias(String) that returns a copy of Artist with an
alias"""  ! testAlias

    //Code removed for brevity

    def testAlias = {pending}
}
```

Here, ^p is used to visually separate one "paragraph" from another, displaying the testing categories with a clear break. Separating testing categories using ^p is not optimal, as we'll see later, but for now fits the purpose. The end result in the output will also show the separation.

```
48. Waiting for source changes... (press enter to interrupt)
[info] Compiling 1 Scala source to /home/danno/testing_scala_book.git/testings-
cala/target/scala-2.9.2/test-classes...
[info] An artist should have a middle name at construction
[info] + An artist should be able to be constructed with a Option[String] mid-
dle name and
[info]            get it back calling 'middleName'
[info] + An artist should be able to have a full name made of the first and
```

```
last name
[info]            given a first and last name at construction time
[info] + An artist should be able to have a full name made of the first, middle
and last name
[info]              given a first, middle, and last name at construction time
[info]
[info] An artist should have an alias
[info] * method called withAlias(String) that returns a copy of Artist with an
alias PENDING
[info]
[info] Total for specification ArtistAcceptanceSpec
[info] Finished in 266 ms
[info] 4 examples, 0 failure, 0 error, 1 pending (+1)
[info] Passed: : Total 4, Failed 0, Errors 0, Passed 3, Skipped 1
[success] Total time: 5 s, completed Dec 30, 2011 3:36:28 PM
```

Again, remember that ^p decrements the next indentation by 1. If the line is indented 5 levels and is followed by ^p, the next line will be at indentation level 4. To go back to 0, use the end^ tag instead.

```
class ArtistAcceptanceSpec extends Specification { def is =
           "An    artist    should    have    a    middle    name    at    construc-
tion"                                                  ^
       """An artist should be able to be constructed with a Option[String] mid-
dle name and
           get it back calling 'middleName'""" ! makeAnArtistWithMiddle-
Name                                ^
       """An artist should be able to have a full name made of the first and
last name
       given a first and last name at construction time""" ! testFullNameWith-
FirstAndLast                ^
       """An artist should be able to have a full name made of the first, middle
and last name
           given a first, middle, and last name at construction time""" ! test-
FullNameWithFirstMiddleAndLast ^

                        end^
               "An        artist        should        have        an
alias"                                                          ^
       """method called withAlias(String) that returns a copy of Artist with an
alias""" ! testAlias


   def makeAnArtistWithMiddleName = {...}

   def testFullNameWithFirstAndLast =  {...}

   def testFullNameWithFirstMiddleAndLast = {...}

   def testAlias = {pending}
```

Although end^ will end the paragraph, it will not add another line. You can get both by using both an end^ and a ^p, but a combination endp^ marker also creates the desired effect.

You can get even more control over indention through the bt^ or t^ tags. For the sake of example, if the first part of the ArtistAcceptanceSpec was written with a three ^t tags after the end of the initial string, the end result would indent the next line three times.

```
        "An      artist     should     have     a     middle     name     at     construc-
tion"                                              ^ t ^ t ^ t ^
        """"An artist should be able to be constructed with a Option[String] mid-
dle name and
                get it back calling 'middleName'"""  !  makeAnArtistWithMiddle-
Name                                     ^

    //code omitted for brevity
```

The t method that does the work of indenting can also accept an Int (a Scala Int) that indents the next line by the number indicated. Rewriting the short example above with the Int parameter produces:

```
        "An      artist     should     have     a     middle     name     at     construc-
tion"                                              ^ t(3) ^
        """"An artist should be able to be constructed with a Option[String] mid-
dle name and
                get it back calling 'middleName'"""  !  makeAnArtistWithMiddle-
Name                                     ^

    //code omitted for brevity
```

In contrast, ^bt^ backtabs. To manipulate tabs for the subsequent line, the same rules apply, only in reverse.

We'll add what we just covered and create an implementation for aliasTest in ArtistAcceptanceSpec.

```
    package com.oreilly.testingscala

    import org.specs2.Specification

    class ArtistAcceptanceSpec extends Specification { def is =
            "An      artist     should     have     a     middle     name     at     construc-
tion"                                              ^ t(3) ^
        """"An artist should be able to be constructed with a Option[String] mid-
dle name and
                get it back calling 'middleName'"""  !  makeAnArtistWithMiddle-
Name                                     ^

                            p^
        """"An artist should be able to have a full name made of the first and
```

```
last name
          given a first and last name at construction time""" ! testFullNameWith-
FirstAndLast                          ^
        """An artist should be able to have a full name made of the first, middle
and last name
             given a first, middle, and last name at construction time""" ! test-
FullNameWithFirstMiddleAndLast ^

                              endp^
                      "An       artist     should      have      an
alias"                                                             ^
        """method called withAlias(String) that returns a copy of Artist with an
alias""" ! testAlias


    def makeAnArtistWithMiddleName = {
      val vaughn = new Artist("Stevie", "Ray", "Vaughn")
      vaughn.middleName must be_==(Some("Ray"))
    }

    def testFullNameWithFirstAndLast = {
      val luther = new Artist("Luther", "Vandross")
      luther.fullName must be_==("Luther Vandross")
    }

    def testFullNameWithFirstMiddleAndLast = {
      val bonJovi = new Artist("Jon", "Bon", "Jovi")
      bonJovi.fullName must be_==("Jon Bon Jovi")
    }

    def testAlias = {
          val theEdge = new Artist("David", "Howell", "Evans").withAlias("The
  Edge")
          theEdge.alias must be_==(Some("The Edge"))
    }
}
```

The result of the test-driven development will in turn cause changes in the Artist
production code—notably, the new withAlias method and a change in the main constructor, as well as the call to that constructor from the auxiliary constructors.

```
package com.oreilly.testingscala

case class Artist(firstName: String, middleName: Option[String], lastName:
String, albums: List[Album], alias:Option[String]) extends Act {
   def this(firstName: String, lastName: String) = this (firstName, None, last-
Name, Nil, None)

   def this(firstName: String, middleName: String, lastName: String) = this
(firstName, Some(middleName), lastName, Nil, None)

   def getAlbums = albums
```

```
    def addAlbum(album: Album) = new Artist(firstName, middleName, lastName, al-
  bum :: albums, alias)

    def fullName = middleName match {
      case Some(x) => firstName + " " + x + " " + lastName
      case _ => firstName + " " + lastName
    }

    def withAlias(alias:String) = new Artist(firstName, middleName, lastName, al-
  bums, Some(alias))
```

Chaining Tests

Each test in specs can be chained to hand off calls and functions to another. This should
be no surprise, since the acceptance specification is merely a collection of objects of the
`Result` type, or `Strings` and methods that return a `Result` type. There is nothing particularly magical about acceptance specifications.

Given/When/Then

In ScalaTest, `GivenWhenThen` structures were in the form of an `Informer`, an object
whose only job is to output any extra information to the end report of the test suite. In
Specs2, `GivenWhenThen` takes on a totally different role. Within the `AcceptanceSpec`,
`GivenWhenThen` is a `Result` fragment object that holds states—one possible state being
`Given`, another `When`, and the final one `Then`—and it passes that state on through to the
test. GWTs are built by inserting GWT "steps" between the textual descriptions and that
those steps keep the state of the current execution and are eventually translated to regular
Text, Step, and Example fragments. Each object is in charge of taking in some data—
either from the previous state or from a `String` specification—and creating another
object, then passing that object on like a baton in a relay race.

`GivenWhenThen` in Specs2, as in ScalaTest, is used to mentally reinforce the definition of
the test into distinct ideas. The examples in this section will be done in parts, due to a
somewhat steep learning curve. The first example shows the basic parts of the test
without the supporting objects it requires.

```
    package com.oreilly.testingscala

    import org.specs2.Specification

    class GivenWhenThenAcceptanceSpec extends Specification { def is = {
        "Demonstrating a Given When Then block for a Specs2 Specification".title ^
        "Given the first name ${David} and the last ${Bowie} create an Artist" ^
    setUpBowie ^
        "When we add the artist to an album called ${Hunky Dory} with the year
    ${1971}" ^ setUpHunkyDory ^
        "And when an the album is added to a jukebox" ^ addTheAlbumToAJukebox ^
```

```
    "Then the jukebox should have one album whose name is ${Hunky Dory}" ^ re-
  sult

      object setUpBowie
      object setUpAlbum
      object addTheAlbumToAJukebox
      object result
  }
```

Let's take the example a little bit at a time. The class declaration and the is method have been covered already in the previous sections. The first string is the title of the test, and is marked as such by the title method.

The second statement is the Given statement. The words *David* and *Bowie*, which are encased in ${}, will be used in the setUpBowie object to create an Artist that will passed down the test.

The next statement, setUpHunkyDory, will take the words *Hunky Dory* and 1971, which are also encased in ${} and use them to create an Album that will be passed down the test. The following statement will add an album to a JukeBox. A jukebox instance will be created and passed down to the last link of the specification. This link will do the final expectations and return a proper Result.

The example ends by defining objects that will parse the contents of ${} and spit out the appropriate objects for the other specification links to take and return the results needed by the next test in sequence.

The next example extends the Given, When, and Then parent classes with appropriate type parameters. This should show how the analogy "passing the baton in a relay race" is appropriate.

```
  //Code removed for brevity
  object setUpBowie extends Given[Artist]
  object setUpHunkyDory extends When[Artist, Album]
  object addTheAlbumToAJukebox extends When[Album, JukeBox]
  object result extends Then[JukeBox]
  //Code removed for brevity
```

Now, the Given, When, and Then rules are in place with their type parameters. The type parameters are the key to understanding how to use GivenWhenThen constructs. First, setUpBowie is used as the Given object. The type parameter is the return parameter, and states that it should return an object of type Artist. Since the Given object returns Artist, there must be either a When object or a Then object that accepts an Artist as its first type parameter, and setUpHunkyDory will answer that call.

setUpHunkyDory is a When object that has two type parameters (as all When objects must). In this case, the first is the type created by the previous link Given object, Artist. The second is the type returned by this object, in this case an Album. In short, setUpHunky Dory will take in an Artist and return an Album.

Next in the chain is a When[Album, Jukebox] object that will take in an Album, the one being returned by setUpHunkyDory, and return an instance of a JukeBox. The final link in the chain is result, which is an object that will take the last object created in this relay race, the Jukebox created by addTheAlbumToAJukebox.

For the beginner, it might be a good idea to start out with the objects to see how they work and use what is learned to sculpt the specifications accordingly.

```
object setUpBowie extends Given[Artist] {
  def extract(text: String) = {
    val tokens = extract2(text)
    new Artist(tokens._1, tokens._2)
  }
}
```

In setUpHunkyDory, the object extends When with parameter types Artist and Album. This indicates that the previous step must return an Artist and that the setUpHunky Dory object must return an Album. The extract method in the object is slightly different because it takes two parameters. The first is the Artist that was returned from the Given case, and the second is the text of the specification. Here extract2 is used to parse out the values into a tuple with the values HunkyDory and 1971. Since an Album is the return type (again, because it's listed as the second type parameter of When), the last line of the extract method will return a new Album using the information parsed and the Ar tist object that was passed down.

```
object setUpHunkyDory extends When[Artist, Album] {
  def extract(p: Artist, text: String) = {
    val tokens = extract2(text)
    new Album(tokens._1, tokens._2.toInt, p)
  }
}
```

For addTheAlbumToAJukebox the object also extends a When with the type parameters Album and Jukebox. In this implementation, extracting the text isn't required since the specification string doesn't contain any required data. The only requirement is the Album that was returned by the previous object, setUpHunkyDory. With that album, a new JukeBox is instantiated and the album is added and returned for the next object to use.

```
object addTheAlbumToAJukebox extends When[Album, JukeBox] {
  def extract(p: Album, text: String) = new JukeBox(Some(List(p)))
}
```

The final link is the `result` object, which extends the `Then` abstract class. The type parameter is the type that is required from the previous object, `addTheAlbumToAJuke` box, which of course is an `Album` type. The `extract` method is the same as it was from the `When` class. The first parameter is the object passed down, and the second text parameter is the `String` from its accompanying specification string. The difference between extending `When` and extending `then` is that the return type in the `Then` class has to be a `Result` type since that is the last element of the chain. In the following example, the `Result` returned is the expectation that the albums in the jukebox total to 1.

```
object result extends Then[JukeBox] {
  def extract(t: JukeBox, text: String) = t.albums.get must have size (1)
}
```

The `GivenWhenThen` specification takes a little work to understand, but once the test developer gets a thorough understanding of how the return types pass results down the chain, the structure becomes self-explanatory, useful, and at times reuseable.

The end result for the previous `GivenWhenThen` example should return the following:

```
[info] Given the first name David and the last Bowie create an Artist
[info] When we add the artist to an album called Hunky Dory with the year 1971
[info] And when an the album is added to a jukebox
[info] + Then the jukebox should have one album whose name is Hunky Dory
[info]
[info] Total for specification Demonstrating a Given When Then block for a
Specs2 Specification
[info] Finished in 26 ms
[info] 1 example, 0 failure, 0 error
[info] Passed: : Total 1, Failed 0, Errors 0, Passed 1, Skipped 0
[success] Total time: 2 s, completed Jan 3, 2012 2:54:47 PM
```

Data Tables

Data tables are ASCII tables that contain sample values and the end result. Once the table is established, a function test case is attached to the end to verify that all the values provided match the criteria. In the following example, we'll show a test that makes sure the date of an album's release matches the age correctly.

```
package com.oreilly.testingscala

import org.specs2.Specification
import org.specs2.matcher.DataTables

class AlbumAgeDataTableSpecification extends Specification with DataTables {def
is =
  "Trying out a table of values for testing purposes to determine the age of
albums".title ^
    """The first column is the album name, the second is a band name,
        and third is a year, and the fourth is the age from the year 2070""" !
```

```
ageTable

  def ageTable =
    "Album Name"          | "Band Name"                | "Year" | "Age" |
    "Under the Iron Sea"  !! "Keane"                    ! 2006   !   64  |
    "Rio"                 !! "Duran Duran"              ! 1982   !   88  |
    "Soul Revolution"     !! "Bob Marley & the Wailers" ! 1971   !   99  |> {
        (a:String, b:String, c:Int, d:Int) ⇒ new Album(a, c, new Band(b)).age-
From(2070) must_== d
      }
}
```

The class definition is an acceptance specification with the inclusion of a DataTables
trait. The DataTable trait contains case classes and methods that makes the data table
magic happen. The example just shown has delineators, the same overall setup as we've
seen in the past: a def declaration, a title, a string specification, and a call to
some Result object or method that returns a Result. What is different, of course, is the
data table.

After the def ageTable = method declaration, the first line contains header information
for the test, delineated by a | pipe character. Each subsequent row of data takes different
delineators, either a ! ! or a ! to delineate each column. The exception is the last column
of each row, because the end of the row is marked with another | pipe character. A data
table can go indefinitely until the a row is terminated with |>, at which point the table
is going to be executed and returned with a Result.

Each column is sent into the function in the form of a Tuple. Since there are four columns
in our table, it will require a Tuple4 parameter that receives each row of data. The
function receives the album name as a string, the band name as a string, the year as an
Int, and the expected Age as an Int. For each row of data, the function will create an
Album, assign the name and year, and create a Band object from the second column. Then
it calls a method called ageFrom, which does not yet exist, that takes the current year
and returns the age of the album as an Int. Finally, an expectation checks whether the
age returned equals the fourth column of the data table, Age.

The use of the current year in the method is intentional. It's a good idea not to use the
current year in actual production code because the year constantly changes. That means
that any test is likely to fail over time. The next year will likely kill all your unit tests.
Having consistent unit tests is not the only reason why the current year, or any temporal
information, should not be calculated in actual production code. The other good reason
is that it makes the code less reusable. If, for instance, there is a requirement to calculate
future statistics on code, it seems a lot of work to redo the guts of a class or object and
extract the current date just to do some forecasting. It's nice to leave such hard dependencies out and plug in what is needed when it is needed.

The results of the test after changing production code are as follows.

```
[info] Compiling 1 Scala source to /home/danno/testing_scala_book.git/testings-
cala/target/scala-2.9.2/test-classes...
[info] + The first column is the album name, the second is a band name,
[info]      and third is a year, and the fourth is the age from the year 2070
[info]
[info] Total for specification Trying out a table of values for testing purpos-
es to determine the age of albums
[info] Finished in 108 ms
[info] 1 example, 0 failure, 0 error
[info] Passed: : Total 1, Failed 0, Errors 0, Passed 1, Skipped 0
[success] Total time: 2 s, completed Jan 3, 2012 2:51:46 PM
```

The changes to the production code include the addition of ageFrom.

```
package com.oreilly.testingscala

class Album(val title: String, val year: Int, val tracks: Option[List[Track]],
val acts: Act*) {

  require(acts.size > 0)

  def this(title: String, year: Int, acts: Act*) = this (title, year, None,
acts: _*)

  def ageFrom(now: Int) = now - year
}
```

Tagging

Specs2 also has a tagging feature that allows the developer to categorize tests. Categorization of tests can be used in both in a unit specification and an acceptance specification. Tests can be filtered in SBT or in the specification itself in case you wish to create
one specification that would run other specifications. The example below is an acceptance specification that uses tags to denote a category for the test. The first specification
in the test is categorized with the strings "timeLength" and "threeTracks". The second
test is categorized also with the String "timeLength" and with "zeroTracks". In order
to make these work, you must import the trait org.specs2.specification.Tags and
add that trait to the specification. In the example below, with Tags is added to the
specification.

```
import org.specs2.Specification
import org.specs2.specification.Tags
import org.joda.time.Period

class Specs2TagAcceptanceSpecification extends Specification with Tags {
  def is =
    "The total time of an album is based on the sum of the tracks".title ^
        "When an album is given three tracks" ! testThreeTracks ^ tag("time-
Length", "threeTracks") ^
        "When an album is given zero tracks" ! testZeroTracks ^ tag("timeLength",
```

```
"zeroTracks")

  def testThreeTracks = {
    val beyonceFirstAlbum = new Album("Dangerously in Love", 2003,
      Some(List(
        new Track("Crazy In Love", "3:56"),
        new Track("Naughty Girl", "3:29"),
        new Track("Baby Paul", "4:05")
      )), new Artist("Beyonce", "Knowles"))
    beyonceFirstAlbum.period must be_== (new Period(0, 10, 90, 0))
  }

  def testZeroTracks = {
      val frankZappaAlbum = new Album("We're only in it for the Money", 1968,
  None, new Band("The Mothers of Invention"))
    frankZappaAlbum.period must be_== (Period.ZERO)
  }
}
```

To run the test using tags in SBT use test-only or ~test-only with the name of the test followed by -- include, with the name of the tags that you wish to run delimited with a comma. For example, to run only zeroTracks tests from the Specs2TagAcceptanceSpecification, the following command line would work:

```
> test-only  com.oreilly.testingscala.Specs2TagAcceptanceSpecification  --  in-
clude zeroTracks
[info] + When an album is given zero tracks
[info]
[info] Total for specification The total time of an album is based on the sum
of the tracks
[info] Finished in 145 ms
[info] 1 example (+1), 0 failure, 0 error
[info] Passed: : Total 1, Failed 0, Errors 0, Passed 1, Skipped 0
[success] Total time: 1 s, completed Jan 4, 2012 2:57:31 PM
```

Again it is worth noting that --include can accept any number of tag keywords, and every test that contains the tags specified will run. In the next example, we show that we are including the tags zeroTracks, completeAlbums, classical, and short-tests to the list of tests that we wish to include.

```
> test-only  com.oreilly.testingscala.Specs2TagAcceptanceSpecification  --  in-
clude zeroTracks completeAlbums classical short-tests
[info] + When an album is given zero tracks
[info]
[info] Total for specification The total time of an album is based on the sum
of the tracks
[info] Finished in 94 ms
[info] 1 example, 0 failure, 0 error
[info] Passed: : Total 1, Failed 0, Errors 0, Passed 1, Skipped 0
[success] Total time: 1 s, completed Jan 4, 2012 3:04:24 PM
```

Fixtures

Fixtures, the ability to call a start method and a close method for a test class mostly standard Scala programming features. Depending on what kind of test you are using, there are different ways to create fixtures. Specs2 tends to take the idealistic stance that most of what you need to do can be achieved using Scala. Let's take a first example of using a mutable list that is shared by two tests in a `Specification`.

```
class Specs2WithoutFixtures extends Specification { def is =
  "Add an album to a shared list" ! test1 ^
  "Remove an album to a shared list" ! test2

  lazy val lst = scala.collection.mutable.Buffer(
    new Album("Fly By Night", 1974, new Band("Rush")),
        new Album("19", 2008, new Artist("Adele", "Laurie", "Adkins").withA-
lias("Adele")))

  def test1 = {
    lst.append(new Album("Prokofiev and Rachmaninoff: Cello Sonatas", 1991, new
Artist("Yo", "Yo", "Ma")))
    lst must have size(3)
  }

  def test2 = lst.drop(1) must have size(1)
}
```

In the above example, `test1` uses the shared list `mutable lst` and appends one album by Yo Yo Ma to that list. After `test1` is run since according to our spec "Add an album to a shared list" starts first. "Remove an album to a shared list" starts next. Each test, as you can tell, was written with the assumption that either the `lst` provided would be unique to the test and not shared. If this test is run, then failure will occur because the `lst` is shared across `test1` and `test2`, and `test2` fails because we were assuming that the `lst` originally had two items.

```
> test-only com.oreilly.testingscala.Specs2WithoutFixtures
[info] Compiling 1 Scala source to /home/danno/testing_scala_book.svn/testings-
cala/target/scala-2.9.2/test-classes...
[info] + Add an album to a shared list
[error] x Remove an album to a shared list
[error]    'Album[19], Album[Prokofiev and Rachmaninoff: Cello Sonatas]' doesn't
have size 1 but size 2 (Specs2CaseClassContext.scala:13)
[info]
[info] Total for specification Specs2WithoutFixtures
[info] Finished in 143 ms
[info] 2 examples, 1 failure, 0 error
```

This is because in this specification we have a shared mutable state. How do we go about creating a unique list for each test? Perhaps the easiest and most functional way is to make the `lst` an immutable data structure which is the default.

```
class Specs2WithoutFixturesButImmutable extends Specification { def is =
  "Add an album to a shared list" ! test1 ^
  "Remove an album to a shared list" ! test2

  lazy val lst = List(
    new Album("Fly By Night", 1974, new Band("Rush")),
      new Album("19", 2008, new Artist("Adele", "Laurie", "Adkins")).withA-
lias("Adele")))

  def test1 = {
    val result = lst :+ new Album("Prokofiev and Rachmaninoff: Cello Sonatas",
1991, new Artist("Yo", "Yo", "Ma"))
    result must have size(3)
  }

  def test2 = lst.drop(1) must have size(1)
}
```

Another score for immutability. So shared state is often the least of your worries with immutability. Let's say that although there may be teams where you do have to manage shared states across tests, or you require a method to initialize a database or a service, having a setup and teardown method (using JUnit parlance) is needed. Given the shared state example Specs2WithoutFixtures above, a set up method can be established using a Scope trait in either a unit specification or an acceptance specification. In an acceptance specification all that is required is a trait that extends Scope and extends that trait in a case class that envelops all tests that require the scoped setup.

```
class Specs2WithScope extends Specification { def is =
  "Add an album to a shared list" ! AddItemTest().test ^
  "Remove an album to a shared list" ! RemoveItemTest().test

  trait ListMaker {
    lazy val lst = scala.collection.mutable.Buffer(
      new Album("Fly By Night", 1974, new Band("Rush")),
        new Album("19", 2008, new Artist("Adele", "Laurie", "Adkins")).withA-
lias("Adele")))
  }

  case class AddItemTest() extends ListMaker {
    def test = {
      lst.append(new Album("Prokofiev and Rachmaninoff: Cello Sonatas", 1991,
new Artist("Yo", "Yo", "Ma")))
      lst must have size(3)
    }
  }

  case class RemoveItemTest() extends ListMaker {
    def test = lst.drop(1) must have size(1)
  }
}
```

Each case class will have one or more test methods in it. Each case class `AddItemTest()` and `RemoveItemTest()` extends from `ListMaker`, which is a trait. The reason a trait works is that its state is unique to each class that extends it. Therefore `AddItemTest()` and `RemoveItemTest` will each have its own list to test.

How do we achieve the same thing for a unit specification? Remember that a unit specification is a specification like its sibling `AcceptanceSpecification` but with a different form. Instead of calling methods from the specification, the tests are run within an `in` clause. Below is the same test as the acceptence specifications that we have been using, but restructured as a unit specification.

```
import org.specs2.mutable.Specification
import org.specs2.specification.Scope


class Specs2UnitSpecificationFixtures extends Specification {
  "Add an album to a shared list" in new ListMaker {
    lst.append(new Album("Prokofiev and Rachmaninoff: Cello Sonatas", 1991, new
Artist("Yo", "Yo", "Ma")))
    lst must have size (3)
  }
  "Remove an album to a shared list" in new ListMaker {
    lst.drop(1) must have size (1)
  }

  trait ListMaker extends Scope {
    lazy val lst = scala.collection.mutable.Buffer(
      new Album("Fly By Night", 1974, new Band("Rush")),
        new Album("19", 2008, new Artist("Adele", "Laurie", "Adkins").withA-
lias("Adele")))
  }
}
```

By now all the players should be familiar, except now each of the tests are inline with the specification, and after the `in` clause we instantiate an anonymous trait that will make available a unique `lst` of albums for each test. This is what we want. But to actually make this work, each trait that must extend 'org.specs2.specification.Scope` in order for Specs2 to understand that the trait will return `Result` type, which is required by the framework. Without extending the `Scope` trait, Specs2 will complain that it cannot implicitly convert a `ListMaker` into a `org.specs2.execute.Result`.

For teardown or cleanup methods, each specification has its own way of doing things. In the unit specification, you continue to use the trait strategy but instead of using `Scope` you use the `org.specs2.mutable.After` trait, which will give a method for you to override—-appropriately called `after`. The `after` method will be called by Specs2 when the test is completed, whether the test fails or succeeds. This next example uses the same data as the previous example but uses the `After` trait instead of the `Scope` trait.

```
class Specs2UnitSpecificationWithAfter extends Specification {
  "Add an album to a shared list" in new ListMaker {
    lst.append(new Album("Prokofiev and Rachmaninoff: Cello Sonatas", 1991, new
Artist("Yo", "Yo", "Ma")))
    lst must have size (3)
    def after {printf("Final tally: %d\n", lst.size)}
  }

  "Remove an album to a shared list" in new ListMaker {
    lst.drop(1) must have size (1)
    def after {printf("Final tally: %d\n", lst.size)}
  }

  trait ListMaker extends After {
    lazy val lst = scala.collection.mutable.Buffer(
      new Album("Fly By Night", 1974, new Band("Rush")),
        new Album("19", 2008, new Artist("Adele", "Laurie", "Adkins")).withA-
lias("Adele")))
  }
}
```

Since After requires that we implement an after method that returns Any object, we
can define an after method in each anonymous instantiation of ListMaker for every
test that we run. In each of tests, the after method returns Unit, which is a type that
represents what void is in Java, C, and C+. This can be refactored though: since
the implementation of +after is the same across multiple tests we can move that
down to the ListMaker trait, where it will look cleaner and still run successfully.

```
class Specs2UnitSpecificationWithAfter extends Specification {
  "Add an album to a shared list" in new ListMaker {
    lst.append(new Album("Prokofiev and Rachmaninoff: Cello Sonatas", 1991, new
Artist("Yo", "Yo", "Ma")))
    lst must have size (3)
  }

  "Remove an album to a shared list" in new ListMaker {
    lst.drop(1) must have size (1)
  }

  trait ListMaker extends After {
    lazy val lst = scala.collection.mutable.Buffer(
      new Album("Fly By Night", 1974, new Band("Rush")),
        new Album("19", 2008, new Artist("Adele", "Laurie", "Adkins")).withA-
lias("Adele")))
    def after {printf("Final tally: %d\n", lst.size)}
  }
}
```

Below are the results of the run. The final tallies are printed after the tallies are run. The
test reporting occurs after the tests have run.

```
> test-only com.oreilly.testingscala.Specs2UnitSpecificationWithAfter
[info] Compiling 1 Scala source to /home/danno/testing_scala_book.svn/testings-
cala/target/scala-2.9.2/test-classes...
Final tally: 3
Final tally: 2
[info] + Add an album to a shared list
[info] + Remove an album to a shared list
[info]
[info] Total for specification Specs2UnitSpecificationWithAfter
[info] Finished in 147 ms
[info] 2 examples, 0 failure, 0 error
[info] Passed: : Total 2, Failed 0, Errors 0, Passed 2, Skipped 0
[success] Total time: 2 s, completed Jan 5, 2012 10:49:04 AM
```

There are multiple solutions for creating fixtures in Specs2. Specs2 has an Around trait that can do the same as previous examples. What is different with the Around trait is that there is one place where a programmer can create logic to be *wrapped* around the test. You may find the trait is similar to either an JavaEE Interceptor or a servlet specification Filter. The recipe for the Around trait is to first do setup, then call the test, which is given as a function parameter, and when the function parameter returns, perform any cleanup that is required.

The object below logs the start and stop of the test. It's a simple fixture. The example uses a simple println to output before and after messages when the test is run. Between each of the outputs, the test is run by calling t, and the result is captured in a variable, result. That reference is held until the end of the test, when it is returned.

```
object log extends org.specs2.specification.Around {
  def around[T <% Result](t: =>T):Result = {
    println("Start process")
    val result:T = t
    println("End process")
    result
  }
}
```

What can be very confusing is the [T <% Result]. This is Scala's type bounds, if there is a converter in the scope of this object that can convert any type T into a Result. That means whatever the type T is, it either has to be a type that *is* of type Result *or* it is of type of something that can be converted into a type Result. The log extends the org.specs2.specification.Around trait which mandates that the method def around be declared. The def around method accepts a function parameter of type Unit=>T, which of course can be shortened to =>T. As a reminder, Unit is the equivalent of a void in Java.

Below we run the test using the log Around trait to do our println log of the test in an acceptance specification. In the specification, we run not just e1 but log(e1). This will wrap the log object around the test method so that when the test runs the around method in the log will run.

```
class UsingTheAroundProcess extends Specification {
  def is =
    "this will log something before running" ! log(e1)

  lazy val lst = List(
    new Album("Storms of Life", 1986, new Artist("Randy", "Travis")),
    new Album("The Bad Touch", 1999, new Band("Bloodhound Gang")),
    new Album("Billie Holiday Sings", 1952, new Artist("Billie", "Holiday")))

  def e1 = {
    println("Running test")
    lst.drop(1) must have size (2)
  }
}
```

Running the above test, we find that everything falls into place. Start Process is invoked first, Running Test is next, and finally End Process is displayed. The advantage of using an Around trait is that this is now extremely reusable. The object can be used in other test methods in other tests.

One of the disadvantages of using an Around trait is that you cannot get access to the state of objects that have been declared inside of the trait. If you establish anything like a service and database, or any object state, you cannot get access to it. If you need this kind of functionality, the Outside trait is useful for declaring a stateful object that needs to instantiated and set up before the test runs. Once the object is set, it can then be delivered to the tester in a function parameter.

 Please don't use external services or databases in unit tests or test-driven development. That is reserved for integration testing or functional testing.

The next example uses the Outside trait to set up a Joda-Time DateTime object that provides the current date and time to the test. The withCurrentDate object extends the Outside trait with the parameterized type DateTime—the type that is the focus the trait. Extending the trait requires the outside method to be declared, which should return the object to be used inside the test. In our example, that is the current DateTime.

```
object withCurrentDate extends org.specs2.specification.Outside[DateTime] {
  def outside = new DateTime
}
```

For good measure we will also include a `withFakeDate` object that is also used inside a test, although this `Outside` trait will return a fixed date of January 2, 1980.

```
object withFakeDate extends org.specs2.specification.Outside[DateTime] {
    def outside = new DateMidnight(1980, 1, 2).toDateTime
}
```

Now we can use these objects inside a test, and much like the `Around` trait, we can use the `Outside` trait nearly the same way, except that it will provide information before running the test. In the next example, `UsingDates` is also an acceptance specification. Instead of calling the test method `testDate` straight away, it is wrapped with the `Out side` trait that provides the needed date. Each specification is given a different date but calls one test method with each of those different dates.

```
class UsingDates extends Specification {def is =

    "this will use the real date" ! (withCurrentDate(x => testDate(x))) ^
    "this will use a fake date" ! (withFakeDate(x => testDate(x)))

    def testDate(x: DateTime) = (x.plusDays(20).isAfterNow)
}
```

This test will run for the top specification but not the bottom one, since the arithmetic doesn't add up.

```
[info] Compiling 1 Scala source to /home/danno/testing_scala_book.svn/testings-
cala/target/scala-2.9.2/test-classes...
[info] + this will use the real date
[error] x this will use a fake date
[error]    the value is false (Specs2AcceptanceSpecificationFixtures.scala:145)
[info]
[info] Total for specification UsingDates
[info] Finished in 539 ms
[info] 2 examples, 1 failure, 0 error
[error] Failed: : Total 2, Failed 1, Errors 0, Passed 1, Skipped 0
[error] Failed tests:
[error]     com.oreilly.testingscala.UsingDates
[error]     {file:/home/danno/testing_scala_book.svn/testingscala/}Testing    Scala/
test:test-only: Tests unsuccessful
[error] Total time: 3 s, completed Jan 6, 2012 2:49:55 PM
```

Finally, what if you wish to have the best of both `Around` and `Outside`? Of course there is an `AroundOutside` that provides that specific solution. The following code is a `log WithFakeDateTime` object that extends the `AroundOutside[DateTime]` trait. The trait requires that the tester use both the `outside` and `around` methods. Based on the previous examples, we can infer that `outside` will set up the object that will be used inside the test, and the `around` method will be run around the test method using the same object.

```
object logWithFakeDateTime extends org.specs2.specification.AroundOutside[Date-
Time] {
    def outside = new DateMidnight(1980, 1, 2).toDateTime
```

```
def around[T <% Result](t: ⇒ T) = {
  println(outside + ": Start process")
  val result = t
  println(outside + ": End process")
  result
}
}
```

Now we can make use of this trait inside the test both as an Around and an Outside.

```
class UsingTheAroundOutsideProcess extends Specification {
  def is =
    "this will log something before running" ! logWithFakeDateTime(dateTime ⇒
  e1(dateTime))

  lazy val lst = List(
    new Album("Storms of Life", 1986, new Artist("Randy", "Travis")),
    new Album("The Bad Touch", 1999, new Band("Bloodhound Gang")),
    new Album("Billie Holiday Sings", 1952, new Artist("Billie", "Holiday")))

  def e1(dt: DateTime) = {
    println("Running test at " + dt)
    lst.drop(1) must have size (2)
  }
}
```

In the above example, logWithFakeDateTime is given the function that accepts the DateTime object as a parameter that is created within the OutsideAround object. We use that DateTime object inside the test method since we need it for our test. Remember that this is also the Around trait, so whatever logic that we stated in the around method will be run. The end result will show the full combination.

```
> test-only com.oreilly.testingscala.UsingTheAroundOutsideProcess
[info] Compiling 1 Scala source to /home/danno/testing_scala_book.svn/testings-
cala/target/scala-2.9.2/test-classes...
2012-01-06T15:08:42.147-06:00: Start process
Running test at 2012-01-06T15:08:42.265-06:00
2012-01-06T15:08:42.280-06:00: End process
[info] + this will log something before running
[info]
[info] Total for specification UsingTheAroundOutsideProcess
[info] Finished in 188 ms
[info] 1 example, 0 failure, 0 error
[info] Passed: : Total 1, Failed 0, Errors 0, Passed 1, Skipped 0
[success] Total time: 3 s, completed Jan 6, 2012 3:08:42 PM
```

Analyzing the end result, we find that the first item, 2012-01-06T15:08:42.147-06:00: Start process came from the around method. The around method then ran the test producing , followed by printing 2012-01-06T15:08:42.280-06:00: End process. The test passed and we successfully established a fixture in Specs2.

Specs2 flexes its muscle with the Scala language. Eric Torreborre, the testing framework's author, likes to be pushing the envelope and trying different things to enhance the framework and create more and more functionality for the test-driven developer. This book covers a lot of what Specs2 covers, but it doesn't cover everything, especially since it is constantly being developed.

Which testing to framework to use? This is up to you. But the real answer is why not both? ScalaTest and Specs2 cover different things for different reasons. ScalaTest offers various specs that are clear and easy to use, and that clarity comes from a well-engineered and well-documented framework. You may find that you need to gradually get used to Scala—especially testing in Scala—and you still enjoy JUnit- and TestNG-style tests. You may also find that data tables in Specs2 come in very handy. If you wish to use ScalaMock (covered later in this book), you will really love its integration with ScalaTest. Both frameworks can run ScalaCheck (also covered later) very well too, and it's recipes will help you decide which framework is best for you. Competition always makes its participants better, and I expect that both these frameworks will have a lot to show in the future.

CHAPTER 5

Mocking

As we've discussed previously, one of the basic tenets of test-driven development is that each test has to be isolated. This means that the test doesn't connect to the Internet, a database, or even the production file system. Typically, these foreign systems are represented through some kind of stunt double to the production object. The following definitions of stunt doubles come from Martin Fowler's blog entry Mocks aren't Stubs (*http://martinfowler.com/articles/mocksArentStubs.html*).

Dummy

An object that does nothing except fill in space. Any calls that it receives will neither change anything nor record anything.

Stub

An object that can consume test behavior and generate some result. It is meant to provide precreated answers for the test. Stubs can be used for recording and analysis to determine the number of calls that are made. They typically require more work than dummies, and an abundance of classes need to be created.

Fake

A fake object is a real object that overrides the more difficult stuff by providing a shortcut.

Mock

An object that is given orders to carry out a prescribed set of commands when it is called upon. This is analogous to the stand-in opponent during preparation for a political debate. The opponent would likely be a campaign team member, but she will have a set of answers already prepared to debate the candidate who needs to train for the big event.

Dummy objects have been used extensively in this book. Consider what we did in covering a Specs2 unit specification. In order to test out our Jukebox we created an Album (that's not the dummy); we also created some Track instances to store in the Album (not dummies either). But in order to make the whole thing work we needed an Act, so we added the band Above and Beyond. It wasn't really necessary, except we wanted to put something in the parameter so we could move along with our test.

src/test/java/com/oreilly/testingscala/JukeboxUnitSpec.scala.

```scala
class JukeboxUnitSpec extends Specification {
  "A Jukebox" should {
    """have a play method that returns a copy of the jukebox that selects
      the first song on the first album as the current track""" in {
      val groupTherapy = new Album("Group Therapy", 2011,
        Some(List(new Track("Filmic", "3:49"),
          new Track("Alchemy", "5:17"),
          new Track("Sun & Moon", "5:25"),
          new Track("You Got to Go", "5:34"))), new Band("Above and Beyond"))
      val jukebox = new JukeBox(Some(List(groupTherapy)))
      val jukeboxNext = jukebox.play
      jukeboxNext.currentTrack.get.name must be_==("Filmic")
      jukeboxNext.currentTrack.get.period must be_==(new Period(0, 3, 49, 0))
    }
  }
}
```

For a fake example, let's create a trait called DAO which will persist any object to some sort of datastore, whether it be a file system or a database. This trait will be used throughout the chapter to highlight fakes, stubs, and mocks from different libraries EasyMock, Mockito, and ScalaMock. Since DAO is a trait, it is intended to be mixed into a class with a concrete implementation that is tied to a specific type of datastore. Possible names could be MySQLDAO, Oracle10DAO, MongoDBDAO, etc. Using a trait in this manner also promotes loose decoupling, since there is no strict shotgun marriage to any particular datasource. The DAO trait has one method, persist, whose job is to accept an input parameter is and persist it to a faked, stubbed, or mocked datastore.

src/test/scala/com/oreilly/testingscala/DAO.scala.

```scala
package com.oreilly.testingscala

trait DAO {
  def persist[T](t:T)
}
```

A fake object is a real object but is a substitute for the real thing. Fakes are typically some sort of holder of a byte array or a map that will store any data that is persisted, reread, or manipulated. Fakes can also be in-memory databases that store the data, like HSQLDB (*http://http://hsqldb.org/*) or H2 (*http://www.h2database.com/html/main.html*), which are full-fledged databases that can be datastores in memory. Please consider, though, that for TDD purposes that may still too much work to set up and defeats the purpose of unit test isolation required for test-driven development.

To make the DAO a fake we can either create a DAO object that has an underlying hash table or use an in-memory database. To keep this example short, we will use a Map to store all entries. For all intents, this fake object is actually a DAO, just not a very good one for production purposes since it is just a simple store to handle all transactions. Its raison d'être is to serve the test.

src/test/com/oreilly/testingscala/UsingFakeUnitSpec.scala.

```scala
package com.oreilly.testingscala

import org.specs2.mutable.Specification

class FakeDAO extends DAO {
  var map = Map[Long, Any]()
  var count = 0L

  def persist[T](t: T) {
    map = map + (count -> t)
    count = count + 1
  }

  def persistCount = map.size
}

class UsingFakeUnitSpec extends Specification {
  "When two albums are added to the fake DAO the albums should be stored" in {
    val dao = new DAOStub
    dao.persist(new Album("The Roaring Silence", 1976, new Band("Manfred Mann's
Earth Band")))
    dao.persist(new Album("Mechanical Animals", 1998, new Artist("Marilyn",
"Manson")))
    dao.persistCount must be_==(2)
  }
}
```

In the above DAO, the first class is the fake, and accepts any object to be persisted. The extra method contains a persistCount method that would give us a current count of objects stored. When persist is called, it is handled and mimics the database as we intended. Inside of the fake is a Map object that handles all the entries. A count variable keeps track of the ID count of all entries. It's rough, simple, and not very sexy, but again, it is just meant to serve the test—just as the punching bag is meant to serve the boxer in training.

Next, a Stub object is just an object that has some sort of logic developed into the code for assertion purposes. Sometimes it is easier to create a stub than to fuss with some sort of fake or mocking framework, because you just need something with some canned answers and you need it quick. The stub object can be as light or complex as you wish to develop it. It would be recommended that if it gets too complicated, then it will be time to change it out for a mock instead.

For the stub, here is an example of a DAOStub and a Specs2 Unit Specification that tracks as many times that a persist call is made. The test in the Specification uses the stub, persists two albums and we then assert that the count is 2. This example of course is painfully easy but shows the use of a Stub in testing situations.

src/test/scala/com/oreilly/testingscala/UsingStubUnitSpec.scala.

```scala
package com.oreilly.testingscala

import org.specs2.mutable.Specification

class DAOStub extends DAO {
  var count = 0

  def persist[T](t: T) {
    count = count + 1
  }

  def persistCount = count
}

class UsingStubUnitSpec extends Specification {

  "Create 2 albums that we will persist to a stub DAO" in {
    val dao = new DAOStub
    dao.persist(new Album("The Roaring Silence", 1976, new Band("Manfred Mann's
Earth Band")))
      dao.persist(new Album("Mechanical Animals", 1998, new Artist("Marilyn",
"Manson")))
    dao.persistCount must be_==(2)
  }
}
```

You can argue that the stub looks similar to the fake. Keep in mind that a fake is an actual implementation of the trait or object you are creating a stunt double for, while a stub is a double that can accept your request but will give you canned answers in return.

Earlier I mentioned that if a stub gets too complicated it would be best to move to a mocking framework. The complication in this example would occur if we add more methods to the DAO, or when the intent of each method becomes difficult with a large permutation of scenarios. Let's create another stub where after one persist, the next persist throws some sort of exception. [1]

src/test/com/oreilly/testingscala/UsingStubUnitSpec.scala.

---

1. Many functional programmers shy away from throwing exceptions, opting instead to use a type like Either to establish whether something was successful or not. This example is meant for demonstration purposes.

```scala
package com.oreilly.testingscala

import org.specs2.mutable.Specification

class DAOStubWithExceptionAfterTheFirstPersist extends DAO {
  var alreadyCalledOnce = false

  def persist[T](t: T) {
    if (alreadyCalledOnce) throw new RuntimeException("Unable to store")
    alreadyCalledOnce = true
  }
}

class UsingStubWithExceptionUnitSpec extends Specification {

  "Create 2 albums that we will persist to a stub DAO" in {
    val dao = new DAOStubWithExceptionAfterTheFirstPersist
    dao.persist(new Album("The Roaring Silence", 1976, new Band("Manfred Mann's
Earth Band")))
      dao.persist(new Album("Mechanical Animals", 1998, new Artist("Marilyn",
"Manson"))) must throwA[RuntimeException]
  }
}
```

But a question arises: how many different stub classes would we have to make for every conceivable use case scenario? This is why mocking easily becomes the best solution. Each of the different test doubles—fakes, dummies, and stubs—has benefits and drawbacks. Some criteria to consider include how long each will take, whether you have to handle side effects, whether you are representing a large system, and whether you are representing a system over a network. A rule of thumb is to use stubs and fakes in unit tests if they can be created quickly and can be managed easily. If they do not, there is good reason to put some investment in creating mocks.

EasyMock

EasyMock was the founding father of Java mocking and set the standard for mocking in the JVM. Today it is still highly favored by many TDDers and works great with any Java bytecode language, including Scala.

EasyMock, like other mocking frameworks, can be compared to a rehearsal. Imagine someone who wants to enter a singles bar hoping to attract the right person. The single man or lady may rehearse in the mirror some catchy lines or a flirtatious move. When ready and satisfied with their results, they enter the club and hope they get some positive interaction.

EasyMock works similar by creating the mock, rehearsing the mock with expected behavior, rewinding the behavior back to the beginning, and sending the mock into the test method to act out what was rehearsed. If there are expected results from the rehearsal, then one may verify that expected calls were actually made. Any unexpected calls that were made notify the programmer that the method wasn't expecting the call. Let's look at mocking in relation to a database, because that's the resource one often has to reproduce for a test.

To install EasyMock, add the `easymock` dependency to the *build.sbt* file. The following shows just the dependencies in the file, excluding the rest of it.

```
//Code removed for brevity

libraryDependencies ++= Seq(
  "org.scalatest" % "scalatest_2.9.2" % "1.8" % "test" withSources() withJava-
doc(),
  "joda-time" % "joda-time" % "1.6.2" withSources() withJavadoc(),
  "junit" % "junit" % "4.10" withSources() withJavadoc(),
  "org.testng" % "testng" % "6.1.1" % "test" withSources() withJavadoc(),
  "org.specs2" %% "specs2" % "1.12.3" withSources() withJavadoc(),
  "org.easymock" % "easymock" % "3.1" withSources() withJavadoc())

//Code removed for brevity
```

For our mocks, we will also the DAO trait, as we have done already in this chapter. Here it is again, so you don't have to turn back.

```
package com.oreilly.testingscala

trait DAO {
  def persist[T](t: T)
}
```

EasyMock originally was used to mock only interfaces in Java (which have been replaced by traits in Scala). Newer generations, including the latest EasyMock, can mock actual concrete classes.

The following example tests a class named `JukeboxStorageService`, whose purpose is to persist the contents of a `JukeBox` into any kind of datastore. The `JukeboxStorage Service` requires the help of two DAOs, one that stores an `Album` and another that stores an `Act`, which is the superclass of `Band` and `Artist`. The test case will start off simply so as not to overwhelm you.

src/test/scala/com/oreilly/testingscala/JukeboxStorageServiceEasyMockSpec.scala.

```
package com.oreilly.testingscala

import org.scalatest.matchers.MustMatchers
import org.scalatest.Spec
import org.easymock.EasyMock._

class JukeboxStorageServiceEasyMockSpec extends Spec with MustMatchers {
  describe("A Jukebox Storage Service") {
    it("should use easy mock to mock out the DAO classes") {
```

```
      val daoMock = createMock(classOf[DAO])
    }
  }
}
```

The example creates a mock of the DAO using the `createMock` method, which is a static method of the EasyMock class. (Remember that EasyMock was written in Java, not Scala, if by chance you're wondering where the `static` came from.) The third import statement uses a wildcard of the class to make any Java static methods or Scala object methods available for use within the class. If you don't want to import the method directly for some reason, just import `org.easymock.EasyMock`, and write out the class with each call: `EasyMock.createMock` instead of the lighter alternative used here, `createMock`.

These mocks will be injected into the JukeboxStorageService class, which will be a subject under test that uses the DAO.

The next step is to set up any stubs or concrete models used in the test. The following example creates some Bands and Artists to give to the JukeboxStorageService so it can store that into our (mocked) datastore.

src/test/scala/com/oreilly/testingscala/JukeboxStorageServiceEasyMockSpec.scala.

```
package com.oreilly.testingscala

import org.scalatest.matchers.MustMatchers
import org.scalatest.Spec
import org.easymock.EasyMock._

class JukeboxStorageServiceEasyMockSpec extends FunSpec with MustMatchers {
  describe("A Jukebox Storage Service") {
    it("should use easy mock to mock out the DAO classes") {
      // previous code removed for brevity

      //set up actual values to be used.
      val theGratefulDead: Band = new Band("Grateful Dead")
      val wyntonMarsalis: Artist = new Artist("Wynton", "Marsalis")
      val psychedelicFurs: Band = new Band("Psychedelic Furs")
      val ericClapton: Artist = new Artist("Eric", "Clapton")

      val workingmansDead = new Album("Workingman's Dead", 1970, None, theGrate-
fulDead)
      val midnightToMidnight = new Album("Midnight to Midnight", 1987, None,
psychedelicFurs)
      val wyntonAndClapton = new Album("Wynton Marsalis and Eric Clapton play
the Blues", 2011, None,
        wyntonMarsalis, ericClapton)

      val jukeBox = new JukeBox(Some(List(workingmansDead, midnightToMidnight,
```

```
wyntonAndClapton)))
      }
    }
  }
```

The example creates two bands (Grateful Dead and Psychedelic Furs) and two artists (jazz great Wynton Marsalis and guitar genius Eric Clapton). Next it creates some albums from the four bands and artists to be used in a JukeBox. The last concrete class used in the test is a jukeBox that contains all the Albums.

In the above example, since we've covered the ScalaTest FunSpec already in Chapter 3, I'll focus here on the use of the EasyMock elements. First, a little more detail on DAO. Each DAO is a trait, and createMock instruments that trait to intercept all calls during testing. createMock accepts the name of the class that it will be mocking. As a Scala aside, classOf[DAO] in Scala is the same as AlbumDAO.class in Java: it merely retrieves the class from the type.

For the next step, we need the actual JukeboxStorageService, which requires one DAO parameter at the time of creation. This is where we will provide the DAO mock. In a real-life system, an actual concrete implementation tied to an actual storage system would be used. Since this is test-driven development and we need to be fast, the mocks will take their place.

src/test/scala/com/oreilly/testingscala/JukeboxStorageServiceEasyMockSpec.scala.

```scala
package com.oreilly.testingscala

import org.scalatest.matchers.MustMatchers
import org.scalatest.Spec
import org.easymock.EasyMock._

class JukeboxStorageServiceEasyMockSpec extends FunSpec with MustMatchers {
  describe("A Jukebox Storage Service") {
    it("should use easy mock to mock out the DAO classes") {

      val daoMock = createMock(classOf[DAO])
      //Code omitted for brevity

      //create the subject under test
      val jukeboxStorageService = new JukeboxStorageService(daoMock)
    }
  }
}
```

Next comes the rehearsal. Each mock will be given "lines" that it needs to act out when called upon by the test.

```scala
package com.oreilly.testingscala

import org.scalatest.matchers.MustMatchers
```

```
import org.scalatest.Spec
import org.easymock.EasyMock._

class JukeboxStorageServiceEasyMockSpec extends Spec with MustMatchers {
  describe("A Jukebox Storage Service") {
    it("should use easy mock to mock out the DAO classes") {

      //previous lines omitted for brevity

      //set up expectations
      albumMock.persist(workingmansDead)
      albumMock.persist(midnightToMidnight)
      albumMock.persist(wyntonAndClapton)

      actMock.persist(theGratefulDead)
      actMock.persist(psychedelicFurs)
      actMock.persist(wyntonMarsalis)
      actMock.persist(ericClapton)
    }
  }
}
```

Each mock will need to be told what to expect. AlbumMock should expect that three albums—*Workingman's Dead*, *Midnight To Midnight*, and *Wynton and Clapton*—will be the parameters of persist in the DAO of Album. In the mock for Act, persist is expected to be called for two band—The Grateful Dead and Psychedelic Furs—and two artists—Wynton Marsalis and Eric Clapton. These expectations don't have to happen in order, they merely have to take place for the test to succeed.

When we created the mock for the DAO using val daoMock = createMock(class Of[DAO]), by default, EasyMock will only check that the expectations were run, but not in any particular order, only that they were called. If ordering expectations is important to you, create a mock with createStrictMock instead of createMock. This would instruct EasyMock to expect your expectation in the order that you provide during rehearsal in your test.

Now that each mock has rehearsed its part, it's time to rewind the behavior by calling replay, calling persist on the subject under test jukeboxStorageService, and verifying the results.

```
package com.oreilly.testingscala

import org.scalatest.matchers.MustMatchers
import org.scalatest.Spec
import org.easymock.EasyMock._

class JukeboxStorageServiceEasyMockSpec extends Spec with MustMatchers {
  describe("A Jukebox Storage Service") {
    it("should use easy mock to mock out the DAO classes") {
      //previous line omitted for brevity
```

```
//replay, more like rewind
replay(daoMock)

//make the call
jukeboxStorageService.persist(jukeBox)

//verify that the calls expected were made
verify(daoMock)
      }
    }
  }
```

replay rewinds all the mocks to set out to perform the prescribed actions we rehearsed. jukeboxStorageService.persist is the actual call to the test, as it sends in a juke Box concrete object. The last line verifies that the mocks acted out what was intended. Running the test now will end in failure, so we can now work on satisfying the test. A few minutes later, perhaps something like the following example would be what the JukeboxStorageService class would like with the behavior that satisfies the test.

src/main/scala/com/oreilly/testingscala/JukeboxStorageService.scala.

```
package com.oreilly.testingscala

class JukeboxStorageService(dao:DAO) {
  def persist(jukeBox:JukeBox) {
    jukeBox.albums.getOrElse(Nil).foreach{
      album => dao.persist(album)
      album.acts.foreach(act => dao.persist(act))
    }
  }
}
```

The persist method, at least for this implementation, gets all the albums, if there are any. getOrElse is a method on Option that returns the contents of Some—in this case a list of albums—or generates an empty list Nil if there are no albums. The forEach method, running on the return value of getOrElse, iterates through the list of albums. album => dao.persist(album) takes each album from the albums List and calls persist on the DAO. Finally, for every act associated with the album, each one will be sent to dao for persistence.

Running the JukeboxStorageServiceEasyMockSpec will now succeed.

```
> test-only com.oreilly.testingscala.JukeboxStorageServiceEasyMockSpec
[info] Compiling 1 Scala source to /home/danno/testing_scala_book.svn/testings-
cala/target/scala-2.9.1/classes...
[info] JukeboxStorageServiceEasyMockSpec:
[info] A Jukebox Storage Service
[info] - should use easy mock to mock out the DAO classes
[info] Passed: : Total 1, Failed 0, Errors 0, Passed 1, Skipped 0
[success] Total time: 9 s, completed Jan 7, 2012 11:12:34 PM
```

This introduction to EasyMock has not been specific to Scala, since this technology has been used for years in Java. EasyMock does contain specific support for ScalaTest, which offers easier ways to work EasyMock.

EasyMock with ScalaTest

ScalaTest offers an `EasyMockSugar` trait that turns replaying and verifying into behind-the-scenes affairs, letting the test developer focus on the rehearsal and running the test. The example we established in the previous section is rewritten here but putting into place some of the sugar.

/src/test/scala/com/oreilly/testingscala/JukeboxStorageServiceEasyMockWithSugar-Spec.scala.

```scala
package com.oreilly.testingscala

import org.scalatest.Spec
import org.scalatest.matchers.MustMatchers
import org.scalatest.mock.EasyMockSugar
import org.easymock.EasyMock._

class JukeboxStorageServiceEasyMockWithSugarSpec extends Spec with MustMatchers
with EasyMockSugar {
  describe("A Jukebox Storage Service") {
    it("should use easy mock sugar in ScalaTest") {
      val daoMock = createMock(classOf[DAO])

      //set up actual values to be used.
      val theGratefulDead: Band = new Band("Grateful Dead")
      val wyntonMarsalis: Artist = new Artist("Wynton", "Marsalis")
      val psychedelicFurs: Band = new Band("Psychedelic Furs")
      val ericClapton: Artist = new Artist("Eric", "Clapton")

      val workingmansDead = new Album("Workingman's Dead", 1970, None, theGrate-
fulDead)
      val midnightToMidnight = new Album("Midnight to Midnight", 1987, None,
psychedelicFurs)
      val wyntonAndClapton = new Album("Wynton Marsalis and Eric Clapton play
the Blues", 2011, None,
        wyntonMarsalis, ericClapton)

      val jukeBox = new JukeBox(Some(List(workingmansDead, midnightToMidnight,
wyntonAndClapton)))

      //create the subject under test
      val jukeboxStorageService = new JukeboxStorageService(daoMock)

      expecting {
        daoMock.persist(workingmansDead)
        daoMock.persist(midnightToMidnight)
        daoMock.persist(wyntonAndClapton)
```

```
        daoMock.persist(theGratefulDead)
        daoMock.persist(psychedelicFurs)
        daoMock.persist(wyntonMarsalis)
        daoMock.persist(ericClapton)
      }

    whenExecuting(daoMock) {
      jukeboxStorageService.persist(jukeBox)
    }
  }
 }
}
```

To compare this latest example with the plain ScalaTest/EasyMock example in the previous section, `replay` and `verify` are gone. Their place is taken by some new methods provided by the `EasyMockSugar` trait: `expecting` and `whenExecuting`.

`expecting` is a function block that just offers a visual categorization of what the mocks expect to be passed, all in one tidy place. `whenExecuting` wraps the replaying and verifications without extra effort.

As always, ScalaTest tries here to give its assertions and set up a fluid linguistic flow. The syntactical sugar used for EasyMock is just another way of doing so. Chapter 6 covers ScalaCheck, and even some more nice syntactic sugar to make testing even easier.

Mockito

Mockito is a later-generation testing framework used mostly in Java. One of the distinct differences between Mockito and ScalaTest is that, in Mockito, mocks don't have to be replayed. Mockito was the first framework to have mocking for a concrete class, but since then EasyMock has also included support for class testing. Mockito also offers Hamcrest integration so that each parameter can have a wild card parameter as part of the assertion.

To set up Mockito for use in SBT, merely include the latest Mockito version (1.9.0 at the time of this writing) within the *build.sbt* file.

```
libraryDependencies ++= Seq("org.scalatest" %% "scalatest" % "1.8" % "test"
withSources() withJavadoc(),
  "joda-time" % "joda-time" % "1.6.2" withSources() withJavadoc(),
  "junit" % "junit" % "4.10" withSources() withJavadoc(),
  "org.testng" % "testng" % "6.1.1" % "test" withSources() withJavadoc(),
  "org.specs2" %% "specs2" % "1.12.3" % "test" withSources() withJavadoc(),
  "org.easymock" % "easymock" % "3.1" % "test" withSources() withJavadoc(),
  "org.mockito" % "mockito-core" % "1.9.0" % "test" withSources() withJavadoc())
```

Mockito works well in ScalaTest and Specs2. In Specs2, since all testing must result in something that needs to return a Result type, Mockito requires special tweaking to work well. Luckily, Specs2 offers a host of sugar for Mockito, although ScalaTest does not. This section will use Mockito both in its raw form and with Specs2 special sugars and DSL to manage mocks better.

The process of using Mockito is nearly the same as using EasyMock. Set up the mocks, rehearse the objects, run the test, and verify. There's no replaying or rewinding the mocks. The following example uses Mockito in a Specs2 acceptance specification.

src/test/scala/com/oreilly/testingscala/JukeboxStorageServiceMockitoAcceptanceS-pec.scala.

```scala
package com.oreilly.testingscala

import org.specs2.Specification
import org.mockito.Mockito._

class JukeboxStorageServiceMockitoAcceptanceSpec extends Specification {
  def is = {
    "You can use Mockito to perform Scala mocking" ! useMockitoToMockClasses
  }

  def useMockitoToMockClasses = {
    val daoMock = mock(classOf[DAO])

    //set up actual values to be used.
    val theGratefulDead: Band = new Band("Grateful Dead")
    val wyntonMarsalis: Artist = new Artist("Wynton", "Marsalis")
    val psychedelicFurs: Band = new Band("Psychedelic Furs")
    val ericClapton: Artist = new Artist("Eric", "Clapton")

    val workingmansDead = new Album("Workingman's Dead", 1970, None, theGrate-
fulDead)
    val midnightToMidnight = new Album("Midnight to Midnight", 1987, None, psy-
chedelicFurs)
    val wyntonAndClapton = new Album("Wynton Marsalis and Eric Clapton play the
Blues", 2011, None,
      wyntonMarsalis, ericClapton)

    val jukeBox = new JukeBox(Some(List(workingmansDead, midnightToMidnight,
wyntonAndClapton)))

    //create the subject under test
    val jukeboxStorageService = new JukeboxStorageService(daoMock)

    //no replay

    //make the call
    jukeboxStorageService.persist(jukeBox)
```

```
        //verify that the calls expected were made
        verify(daoMock).persist(theGratefulDead)
        verify(daoMock).persist(workingmansDead)
        success
    }
}
```

Instead of createMock, Mockito uses a mock method to generate the mocks. The sample uses a number of concrete methods available for tests. Again, there is no replay involved. The verification syntax is also very different. The verify method just accepts the mock, at which point another method can be called to verify the behavior. In other words, the last lines of the acceptance specification shown here are of the form verify(mock).meth od(params), where method is the method that is expected to be called and the parameters given are the parameters that were expected to be delivered. If any verification fails, an exception is thrown. For example, one feature of testing frameworks, including Easy-Mock, is that the developer can specify how many times a particular method can be called with a given parameter. The developer is free to explicitly state that a method should never be called, or that a method should be called 10 times.

In Mockito, you can specify the number of times a method should be called with a VerificationMode in the verify method. If, for example, a verification should fail, the last verify statement can be amended to state:

```
verify(albumMock, never()).persist(workingmansDead)
```

Doing so will cause an exception and a test failure—not the nice kind where it shows up in a report but with a visually abhorrent stack trace.

```
[info] Compiling 1 Scala source to /home/danno/testing_scala_book.git/testings-
cala/target/scala-2.9.0-1/test-classes...
[error] x You can use Mockito to perform Scala mocking
[error]
[error] dAO.persist(
[error]     com.oreilly.testingscala.Album@202d0e83
[error] );
[error] Never wanted here:
[error] -> at com.oreilly.testingscala.JukeboxStorageServiceMockitoAcceptanceS-
pec.useMockitoToMockClasses(JukeboxStorageServiceMockitoAcceptanceSpec.scala:38)
[error] But invoked here:
[error] -> at com.oreilly.testingscala.JukeboxStorageService$$anonfun$persist
$2.apply(JukeboxStorageService.scala:7)
[error]   (JukeboxStorageServiceMockitoAcceptanceSpec.scala:8)
[info]
[info] Total for specification JukeboxStorageServiceMockitoAcceptanceSpec
[info] Finished in 192 ms
[info] 1 example, 1 failure (+1), 0 error
[error] Failed: : Total 1, Failed 1, Errors 0, Passed 0, Skipped 0
[error] Failed tests:
```

```
[error]    com.oreilly.testingscala.JukeboxStorageServiceMockitoAcceptanceSpec
[error]    {file:/home/danno/testing_scala_book.git/testingscala/}default-cef86a/
test:test-only: Tests unsuccessful
[error] Total time: 2 s, completed Jan 6, 2012 2:24:06 PM
```

Mockito with Specs2

Specs2 comes with its own Mockito sugar[2] to create the necessary `Result`, and it includes a few language enhancements along the way. The next example revises the acceptance spec shown in the previous section, adding some Specs2 goodness.

```
package com.oreilly.testingscala

import org.specs2.Specification
import org.specs2.mock.Mockito

class JukeboxStorageServiceMockitoSugarAcceptanceSpec  extends  Specification
with Mockito {
  def is = {
    "You can use Mockito to perform Scala mocking" ! useMockitoToMockClasses
  }

  def useMockitoToMockClasses = {
    val daoMock = mock[DAO] as "album mock"

    //set up actual values to be used.
    val theGratefulDead: Band = new Band("Grateful Dead")
    val wyntonMarsalis: Artist = new Artist("Wynton", "Marsalis")
    val psychedelicFurs: Band = new Band("Psychedelic Furs")
    val ericClapton: Artist = new Artist("Eric", "Clapton")

    val workingmansDead = new Album("Workingman's Dead", 1970, None, theGrate-
fulDead)
    val midnightToMidnight = new Album("Midnight to Midnight", 1987, None, psy-
chedelicFurs)
    val wyntonAndClapton = new Album("Wynton Marsalis and Eric Clapton play the
Blues", 2011, None,
      wyntonMarsalis, ericClapton)

    val jukeBox = new JukeBox(Some(List(workingmansDead, midnightToMidnight,
wyntonAndClapton)))

    //create the subject under test
    val jukeboxStorageService = new JukeboxStorageService(daoMock)

    //no replay
```

---

2. The recipe for the mojito beverage, which Mockito is loosely named after, requires a good amount of superfine sugar.

```
        //make the call
        jukeboxStorageService.persist(jukeBox)

        //verify that the calls expected were made
        there was one (daoMock).persist(theGratefulDead)
        there was one (daoMock).persist(workingmansDead)
    }
}
```

The example mixes in the Mockito trait, which provides a different syntax that returns the Result type expected from a Specs2 test. The information in this test is not much different from a regular Mockito-based test, except for the matchers in the last two lines. The matchers use Specs2 language to verify the mock. there was one signifies that there was one call to the method persist with the object reference theGratefulDead on the mock actMock. Much like the other mocking frameworks, any mock can be specified with the number of times it should be called, either on the rehearsal or on the verification. Here we expect that one persist call is made for theGratefulDead and one for their album workingmansDead.

Using the Specs2 Mockito language, the developer can get fairly fancy with how to describe the number of times a particular mock is expected to be called. Some other Specs2 phrases include there was two, and, for those who favor good grammar, there were two. there were three, there were atLeastOne, there were atLeastTwo, there were atMostOne, there were atMostTwo, etc.

Order verification

To specify an order to operations using the Specs2 Mockito language, we set up chaining using a then method. For instance, we could rewrite the specification from the previous section to specify that an order is required, as follows:

```
there was one (actMock).persist(theGratefulDead) then one (albumMock).per-
sist(workingmansDead)
```

ScalaMock

ScalaMock is a mocking framework that is all Scala, and meant for Scala only. Its purpose as a mocking framework is to get into some of the hardest testing spots in Scala, such as functions, singleton objects, companion objects, static methods, final objects, and final methods. ScalaMock can also mock traits and concrete classes like the other mocking frameworks.

ScalaMock was originally called Borachio but has taken on a new name. The original Borachio framework supported only traits and functions, but of late supports a wide range of Scala construct, and is ever-growing. ScalaMock works only with SBT, since it uses an SBT compiler plug-in. This is essential to create an action called *generate-mocks* that is used to create bytecode of the mocks in order to use them.

Using ScalaMock with SBT calls for a bit more setup than most frameworks we've seen. You have to delete the *build.sbt* file in favor of a Scala-based build file. SBT works with two types of build files. One is the *.sbt* file we've seen, a user-friendly format where you can set up dependencies, names, versions and the like. But in order to do something a little more complicated, you instead need a *.scala* build file.

After deleting *build.sbt*, create *project/project/Build.scala* and *project/TestingScala.scala*. The first file will define the compiler plug-in used to generate the mocks, while the second will be the actual build file. Insert the following into */project/project/Build.scala*:

project/project/Build.scala.

```
import sbt._

object PluginDef extends Build {
  override lazy val projects = Seq(root)
  lazy val root = Project("plugins", file(".")) dependsOn(scalamockPlugin)
    lazy val scalamockPlugin = uri("git://github.com/paulbutcher/scalamock-sbt-
  plugin")
}
```

In SBT, these calls register the plug-in to be used within SBT and which projects to attach to. This `Plugin` definition will attach to the root project and retrieve the plug-in from a Git repository.

The new project file, *project/TestingScala.scala*, is the replacement to *build.sbt*. This file identifies some of the usual suspects. But whereas our original *build.sbt* was based on keys and values, this file is pure Scala code and looks like the following.

```
import sbt._
import Keys._
import ScalaMockPlugin._

object TestingScala extends Build {

  override lazy val settings = super.settings ++ Seq(
    organization := "com.oreilly.testingscala",
    version := "1.0",
    scalaVersion := "2.9.2",

    resolvers += ScalaToolsSnapshots,
     resolvers ++= Seq("snapshots" at "http://oss.sonatype.org/content/reposito-
  ries/snapshots",
                      "releases" at "http://oss.sonatype.org/content/reposito-
```

```
ries/releases"),
    libraryDependencies ++= Seq("org.scalatest" %% "scalatest" % "1.8" % "test"
withSources() withJavadoc(),
    "joda-time" % "joda-time" % "1.6.2" withSources() withJavadoc(),
    "junit" % "junit" % "4.10" withSources() withJavadoc(),
    "org.testng" % "testng" % "6.1.1" % "test" withSources() withJavadoc(),
    "org.specs2" %% "specs2" % "1.12.3" % "test" withSources() withJavadoc(),
    "org.easymock" % "easymock" % "3.1" % "test" withSources() withJavadoc(),
    "org.mockito" % "mockito-core" % "1.9.0" % "test" withSources() withJava-
doc(),
    "org.scalamock" %% "scalamock-scalatest-support" % "2.3-SNAPSHOT")),
    autoCompilerPlugins := true,
    addCompilerPlugin("org.scalamock" %% "scalamock-compiler-plugin" % "2.3-
SNAPSHOT"),
    scalacOptions ++= Seq("-deprecation", "-unchecked")),

    lazy val myproject = Project("Testing Scala", file(".")) settings(generate-
MocksSettings: _*) configs(Mock)
}
```

The new build file contains the organization, version, and scalaVersion used for the project. resolvers, as before, are the Maven-based repositories that contain the dependencies. ScalaToolsSnapshots just includes the snapshots repository. ScalaTools Releases is already included implicitly. The OSS Sonatype repositories were needed for Specs2. libraryDependencies, much like in the former *build.sbt*, contains all the dependencies, and there is a new dependency at the end of this Seq, ScalaMock.

Some new settings are included:

autoCompilerPlugins
:   Turns on the compiler plugin functionality.

addCompilerPlugin
:   Specifies which compiler plugin to use.

scalacOptions
:   Are not ScalaMock specific. They are merely compilation flags for the Scala compiler.

The last line of the build file contains the project name, indicates where the the root of the project is located, and adds the generateMockSettings and configuration required to load the mocked classes into the test.

Behind the scenes, ScalaMock creates classes based on the signatures of the classes specified by the developer that need mocking. This will be covered shortly.

To verify that the setup works, run reload and update in SBT, either on the shell command line or in interactive mode.

Mocking Traits

Mocking a trait is the most basic type of mocking, and ScalaMock, of course, supports it. Given the previous mocking examples in the book, for Mockito and EasyMock, the following example demonstrates the use of mocking using ScalaMock. Because Scala-Mock provides its own support for traits, no extra setup is required for this example, but there will be extra setup for subsequent examples that mock other structures.

testingscala/src/test/scala/com/oreilly/testingscala/UsingScalaMockSample.scala.

```
package com.oreilly.testingscala

import org.scalatest.Spec
import org.scalatest.matchers.MustMatchers
import org.scalamock.scalatest.MockFactory
import org.scalamock.generated.GeneratedMockFactory

class UsingScalaMockSample extends Spec with MustMatchers with MockFactory {
  describe("ScalaMocks can create mocks of traits") {
    it("can create a mock for a trait") {
      val daoMock = mock[DAO]

      //set up actual values to be used.
      val theGratefulDead: Band = new Band("Grateful Dead")
      val wyntonMarsalis: Artist = new Artist("Wynton", "Marsalis")
      val psychedelicFurs: Band = new Band("Psychedelic Furs")
      val ericClapton: Artist = new Artist("Eric", "Clapton")

      val workingmansDead = new Album("Workingman's Dead", 1970, theGrateful-
Dead)
      val midnightToMidnight = new Album("Midnight to Midnight", 1987, psychede-
licFurs)
      val wyntonAndClapton = new Album("Wynton Marsalis and Eric Clapton play
the Blues", 2011, wyntonMarsalis, ericClapton)

      val jukeBox = new JukeBox(Some(List(workingmansDead, midnightToMidnight,
wyntonAndClapton)))

      //create the subject under test
      val jukeboxStorageService = new JukeboxStorageService(daoMock)

      daoMock.expects.persist(workingmansDead)
      daoMock.expects.persist(midnightToMidnight)
      daoMock.expects.persist(wyntonAndClapton)

      daoMock.expects.persist(theGratefulDead)
      daoMock.expects.persist(psychedelicFurs)
      daoMock.expects.persist(wyntonMarsalis)
      daoMock.expects.persist(ericClapton)
```

```
        jukeboxStorageService.persist(jukeBox)
  }
}
```

ScalaMock requires the type of the object that is to be mocked. In this example, `mock[DAO]` generates a mock of the DAO class, which is the mocked type. The subsequent lines, as before, are dummy objects for `Bands`, `Artists`, and `Albums` used to test the DAO. Each dummy object is placed into the `JukeBox` object, which will be used inside the `jukeboxStorageService`.

After creating the `JukeboxStorageService`, the expectations on the mock are created. `daoMock` expects that `persist` is called for all three albums: *Workingmans Dead*, *Midnight to Midnight*, and *Wynton and Clapton*. In the next set, expectations are made for the two bands, the Grateful Dead and the Psychedelic Furs. Finally come expectations for the artists, Wynton Marsalis and Eric Clapton.

To invoke the tests, a call to `persist` is made on the `jukeboxStorageService` object. Again, the only difference is the setup. Testing for traits in ScalaMock is similar to EasyMock and Mockito. But where ScalaMock will leave its competitors in the dust is in its ability to test things such as functions, objects, companion objects, final classes, and methods.

Mocking Classes

Like Mockito and EasyMock, ScalaMock can mock concrete classes. To use it, you must run the `generate-mocks` compiler plug-in by calling `generate-mocks` in `sbt` before running your test. `generate-mocks` generates instrumented classes in the *target/scala-version/mock-classes* folder of the project. These classes will be substituted for the real classes during the text. The command also installs a trait named `org.scalamock.gen erated.GeneratedMockFactory`. The trait will be compiled when generated.

Therefore at the time of compilation, the developer will not see this trait as if it is something concrete. For most developers working in IDEs, the trait would be highlighted in some way, such as appearing red.

After the setup has been completed, the shell of the test should look like the following example. When viewing the sample, notice that we include an import statement for `org.scalamock.generated.GeneratedMockFactory` and extend it as a trait.

/src/test/scala/com/oreilly/testingscala/UsingScalaMockSample.scala.

```
package com.oreilly.testingscala

import org.scalatest.Spec
import org.scalatest.matchers.MustMatchers
import org.scalamock.scalatest.MockFactory
import org.scalamock.generated.GeneratedMockFactory
```

```
class UsingScalaMockSample extends Spec with MustMatchers with MockFactory with
GeneratedMockFactory {
    //Put tests here.
}
```

To create a mock for a concrete class, a declaration must be made that the class is to be mocked. In order to achieve that, a new class needs to be created with different categorization.

In the *src* folder of the project, create a folder named *generate-mocks* that is a sibling of *main* and *test*. Within the *generate-mocks* folder, create a folder named *scala*. Within the *scala* folder, which is now a folder on the classpath, a dummy class needs to be created. The name of the class doesn't matter. It is a placeholder for annotations that detail which classes should be mocked and how they should be mocked. Figure 5-1 shows a sample layout for the projects in this book.

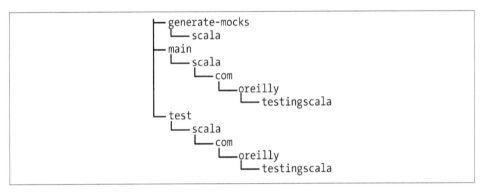

Figure 5-1. Folder arrangement for the generate-mocks folder

In the following example, the placeholder class will be called GenerateMocks. To reemphasize, this class that you create can be called whatever you would like. Above of the dummy class will be annotations for all mocks, companion, and singleton mocks that are required to test the class.

/src/generate-mocks/scala/GenerateMocks.scala.

```
import com.oreilly.testingscala._
import org.scalamock.annotation.{mock}

@mock[Artist]
@mock[Album]
@mock[Track]
class GenerateMocks
```

Once the annotations are in place on the dummy class, ScalaMock will use the annotations to create mock classes that will be used in place of the actual classes. The test for our next example requires mocks for the Artist, Band, and Album classes.

/src/test/scala/com/oreilly/testingscala/UsingScalaMockSample.scala.

```scala
package com.oreilly.testingscala

import org.scalatest.Spec
import org.scalatest.matchers.MustMatchers
import org.scalamock.scalatest.MockFactory
import org.scalamock.generated.GeneratedMockFactory


class UsingScalaMockSample extends Spec with MustMatchers with MockFactory with
GeneratedMockFactory {

  describe("ScalaMocks can create mocks of various structures") {
    //Previous test omitted for brevity

    it("can also mock regular object, and along with other traits") {
      val daoMock = mock[DAO]
      //set up actual values to be used.
      val theGratefulDead: Band = mock[Band]
      val wyntonMarsalis: Artist = mock[Artist]
      val psychedelicFurs: Band = mock[Band]
      val ericClapton: Artist = mock[Artist]

      val workingmansDead = mock[Album]
      val midnightToMidnight = mock[Album]
      val wyntonAndClapton = mock[Album]

      val jukeBox = mock[JukeBox]

      //create the subject under test
      val jukeboxStorageService = new JukeboxStorageService(daoMock)

      inSequence {
        jukeBox.expects.albums returning (Some(List(workingmansDead, midnightTo-
Midnight, wyntonAndClapton)))

        daoMock.expects.persist(workingmansDead)
        workingmansDead.expects.acts returning (List(theGratefulDead))
        daoMock.expects.persist(theGratefulDead)

        daoMock.expects.persist(midnightToMidnight)
        midnightToMidnight.expects.acts returning (List(psychedelicFurs))
        daoMock.expects.persist(psychedelicFurs)

        daoMock.expects.persist(wyntonAndClapton)
        wyntonAndClapton.expects.acts returning (List(ericClapton, wyntonMarsa-
lis))
```

```
        daoMock.expects.persist(ericClapton)
        daoMock.expects.persist(wyntonMarsalis)
    }

    jukeboxStorageService.persist(jukeBox)
  }
}
```

This example creates mocks out of the concrete classes Band, Artist, Album, JukeBox, and DAO. The test class, jukeboxStorageService, lists its assertions in order using the inSequence{..} block. If any of the calls are not made, or if they are made out of order, an org.scalamock.ExpectationException will be thrown. As before, after all the assertions have been made, the method call or calls to the subject under test can be made.

The following sample shows an sbt testing session using ScalaMock. As I mentioned before, you must call generate-mocks in sbt before the test.

```
> clean
[success] Total time: 0 s, completed Mar 15, 2012 8:47:45 PM
> generate-mocks
[info] Updating {file:/home/danno/testing_scala_book.svn/testingscala/}Testing
Scala...
[info] Resolving joda-time#joda-time;1.6.2 ...
[info] Resolving junit#junit;4.10 ...
....
[info] Resolving org.scalamock#scalamock-compiler-plugin_2.9.1;2.3-SNAPSHOT ...
[info] Resolving org.scala-lang#scala-compiler;2.9.1 ...
[info] Done updating.
[info] Compiling 13 Scala sources to /home/danno/testing_scala_book.svn/
testingscala/target/scala-2.9.1/classes...
[log generatemocks] Creating mock for: class Artist
[log generatemocks] Creating mock for: class Artist
....
[log generatemocks] Creating mock for: class Track
[log generatemocks] Creating mock for: class Band
[log parser] parsing Iterator.class
[success] Total time: 25 s, completed Mar 15, 2012 8:48:18 PM
> test:compile
[info] Compiling 19 Scala sources to /home/danno/testing_scala_book.svn/
testingscala/target/scala-2.9.1/mock-classes...
[info] Compiling 52 Scala sources to /home/danno/testing_scala_book.svn/
testingscala/target/scala-2.9.1/test-classes...
[success] Total time: 99 s, completed Mar 15, 2012 8:51:44 PM
> ~test-only com.oreilly.testingscala.UsingScalaMockSample
[info] UsingScalaMockSample:
[info] ScalaMocks can create mocks of various structures
[info] - can create a mock for a trait
[info] - can also mock regular object, and along with other traits
[info] Passed: : Total 2, Failed 0, Errors 0, Passed 2, Skipped 0
[success] Total time: 1 s, completed Mar 15, 2012 8:52:02 PM
1. Waiting for source changes... (press enter to interrupt)
```

It is worth getting into the habit of calling `generate-mocks` each time a change is made to a class that is mocked, since the mock in current use doesn't have the latest updates. Although this is somewhat inelegant now, there should be a more streamlined process in the future.

Mocking Singleton Objects

The strength of ScalaMock doesn't stop there. It can also mock singleton objects. This in itself is perhaps the best selling point for ScalaMock. In the Java space, mocking static methods has often been a pain point for the test-driven developer. Such limitations caused us to rethink our programming structure, and not be so dependent on the `static` keyword, a blessing in disguise. Static methods are not used as heavily today, except for constructs like static factory methods in frameworks like Spring. In Scala, there is no `static` keyword, and therefore no static initializers, variables, or methods. In lieu of `static`, Scala uses `object`. It can be used either as a factory or as a declared instance of a class. A Java programmer coming to Scala can consider the `object` as a structure that houses methods and variables that would have been static in Java.

The following example shows a singleton class for The Boss—`BruceSpringsteenFactory`. The factory is there to create objects or a list of `Album` objects that created Bruce Springsteen. The `artist` method is used to create an `Artist` object representing Bruce. The `discography` method creates a `List` of `Album` objects representing some of his earlier works, and finally the `jukebox` method creates a `JukeBox` object of all of Bruce's work.

/src/main/scala/com/oreilly/testingscala/BruceSpringsteenFactory.scala.

```scala
package com.oreilly.testingscala

object BruceSpringsteenFactory {
  private lazy val theBoss = {
    println("loaded the info");
    new Artist("Bruce", None, "Springsteen", Nil, Some("The Boss"))
  }

  def artist = discography.foldLeft(theBoss) {
    (boss, album) ⇒ boss.addAlbum(album)
  }

  def discography = List(
    new Album("Greetings from Ashbury Park, N.J.", 1973, None, theBoss),
    new Album("The Wild, The Innocent\n& the E Street Shuffle", 1973, None, the-
Boss),
    new Album("Born To Run", 1975, None, theBoss),
    new Album("Darkness on the Edge of Town", 1978, None, theBoss),
    new Album("The River", 1980, None, theBoss),
    new Album("Nebraska", 1982, None, theBoss),
```

```
      new Album("Born in the USA", 1984, None, theBoss))

    def jukebox = new JukeBox(Some(discography))
  }
```

What if this object is used within another object that happens to be the subject under test? That would make BruceSpringsteenFactory a prime candidate to be mocked. The next example is a test for a class named BruceSpringsteenStatistics, another object that provides statistics for Bruce Springsteen given the information provided by the singleton, BruceSpringsteenFactory.

/src/test/scala/com/oreilly/testingscala/UsingScalaMockSample.scala.

```
package com.oreilly.testingscala

import org.scalatest.Spec
import org.scalatest.matchers.MustMatchers
import org.scalamock.scalatest.MockFactory
import org.scalamock.generated.GeneratedMockFactory

class UsingScalaMockSample extends Spec with MustMatchers with MockFactory with
GeneratedMockFactory {
  describe("ScalaMocks can create mocks of various structures") {

    //Previous Tests omitted for brevity

    it("can mock a singleton object") {
      val bruceSpringsteenFactory = mockObject(BruceSpringsteenFactory)

      val albumMock1 = mock[Album]
      val albumMock2 = mock[Album]
      val albumMock3 = mock[Album]

      albumMock1.expects.year returning (1978)
      albumMock2.expects.year returning (1990)
      albumMock3.expects.year returning (1999)

        bruceSpringsteenFactory.expects.discography returning List(albumMock1, al-
bumMock2, albumMock3)

        BruceSpringsteenStatistics.numberOfAlbums must be (3)
        BruceSpringsteenStatistics.averageYear must be ((1978 + 1990 + 1999) / 3)
    }
  }
}
```

In this example, BruceSpringsteenFactory is the singleton object to be mocked. BruceSpringsteenStatistics is another singleton, but is the subject under test. The point of the test is to derive the statistics from BruceStringsteenStatistics using test-driven development. mockObject is a method that creates a mock for the singleton. Note that mockObject uses parentheses whereas mock uses brackets. mockObject accepts the singleton as an argument in order to generate the mock.

The next lines create three mock Album objects and three expectations about those mocks: that the first album will return the year 1978, that the second album will return 1990, and that the third will return 1999. Next, the bruceSpringsteenFactory has an expectation that the discography method will be called and will return a list of the Album mocks that have been established. Finally, the last two lines assert that the num berOfAlbums and averageYear method will return the expected results.

Some additional setup is still required. The GeneratedMocks dummy class will need to be notified that the BruceSpringsteenFactory needs to be mocked. The following code snippet does this.

/src/generate-mocks/scala/GenerateMocks.scala.

```scala
import com.oreilly.testingscala._
import org.scalamock.annotation.{mockWithCompanion, mockObject, mock}

@mock[Artist]
@mock[Album]
@mock[Track]
@mock[DAO]
@mock[JukeBox]
@mockObject(BruceSpringsteenFactory)
class GenerateMocks
```

This example is different from the first one in this section in that it uses @mockObject with the singleton as a parameter, instead of @mock, which takes a type parameter.

Now you should run clean, generate-mocks, and test:compile, and then test the class to let a failure happen. Implementing the class and satisfying the test would now somewhat look like the following example.

/src/main/scala/com/oreilly/testingscala/BruceSpringsteenStatistics.scala.

```scala
package com.oreilly.testingscala

object BruceSpringsteenStatistics {
  def numberOfAlbums = BruceSpringsteenFactory.discography.size
  def averageYear = BruceSpringsteenFactory.discography.map(_.year).sum / num-
berOfAlbums
}
```

This is a huge advancement in testing, and the setup required to test tough scenarios like singletons is fairly minimal. For many testers, this is welcoming.

Mocking Companion Objects

In Scala, an object with the same name as a class is called a *companion object*. The role of a companion object is to offer factory methods for the accompanying class or trait and extractors for pattern matching, as well as house shared variables between objects created from the class. A companion object and its associated class also have access to each other's members' variables.

For an example of testing a companion object with ScalaMock, we'll give the DAO trait some company: two classes that are implementations of the DAO trait, and a DAO companion object in charge of doling out the concrete implementations of the DAO.

/src/main/scala/com/oreilly/testingscala/DAO.scala.

```
package com.oreilly.testingscala

trait DAO {
  def persist[T](t:T)
}

object DAO {
  private class MySqlDAO extends DAO {def persist[T](t:T){}}
  private class DB2DAO extends DAO {def persist[T](t:T){}}

  def createMySqlDAO:DAO = new MySqlDAO
  def createDB2DAO:DAO = new DB2DAO
}
```

The DAO object has the same name as the trait, and is therefore a companion to the trait. The companion object has two factory methods, one that will return a MySqlDAO object, and another that will return a DB2DAO object. The following code mocks the companion and hijacks createMySQLDAO and createDB2DAO to return the object that will be defined by the test programmer. The subject under test for the example will be a class called AlbumMultipleStorageService that uses the DAO companion object to obtain the data access objects for two different kinds of databases, one for mySQL, and one for DB2. AlbumMultipleStorageService then will use both of the DAOs to store the Artist, Peter Murphy, and then use both DAOs to store the album, Cascade.

/src/test/scala/com/oreilly/testingscala/UsingScalaMockSample.scala.

```
package com.oreilly.testingscala

import org.scalatest.Spec
import org.scalatest.matchers.MustMatchers
import org.scalamock.scalatest.MockFactory
import org.scalamock.generated.GeneratedMockFactory


class UsingScalaMockSample extends Spec with MustMatchers with MockFactory with
GeneratedMockFactory {
```

```
describe("ScalaMocks can create mocks of various structures") {

  //previous tests omitted for brevity

  it("can mock a companion object") {
    val daoMockCompanion = mockObject(DAO)

    val daoMockMySql = mock[DAO]
    val daoMockDB2 = mock[DAO]

    val peterMurphy: Artist = new Artist("Peter", "Murphy")

    val cascade = new Album("Cascade", 1995, peterMurphy)

    daoMockCompanion.expects.createMySqlDAO returning (daoMockMySql)
    daoMockCompanion.expects.createDB2DAO returning (daoMockDB2)

    inSequence {
      daoMockMySql.expects.persist(cascade)
      daoMockDB2.expects.persist(cascade)
      daoMockMySql.expects.persist(peterMurphy)
      daoMockDB2.expects.persist(peterMurphy)
    }

    val albumMultipleStorageService = new AlbumMultipleStorageService()
    albumMultipleStorageService.persist(cascade);
  }
 }
}
```

mockObject is called with the singleton companion object that needs to be mocked for testing purposes. The DAO companion object will be used inside the AlbumMultipleStorageService to retrieve the two DAOs. After mocking the companion object, a regular trait mock is made for the mySQL DAO, and another for the DB2 DAO. Next, the Artist, Peter Murphy, is created, as well as his album, *Cascade*, with a reference to the artist object. This is followed by expectations of the companion object. The code inside of the inSequence block consists of expectations made to the mySQL and DB2 DAO mocks in the specified sequential order. Finally, the subject under test, AlbumMultipleStorageService, is instantiated, and the persist method is called with the album, *Cascade*.

A change must be made in the dummy class, GenerateMocks, to notify ScalaMock that along with the DAO trait, its companion object will be mocked as well.

```
import com.oreilly.testingscala._
import org.scalamock.annotation.{mockWithCompanion, mockObject, mock}

@mock[Artist]
@mock[Album]
@mock[Track]
```

```
@mock[Band]
@mock[JukeBox]
@mock[CompilationAlbum]
@mockWithCompanion[DAO]
@mockObject(BruceSpringsteenFactory)
class GenerateMocks
```

The significant change is that the annotation is no longer @mock[DAO] but @mockWith
Companion[DAO]. This lets ScalaMock know it must generate a mock with the intent that
not only will the trait or class be mocked, but its corresponding companion object as
well.

After calling generate-mocks in SBT, compiling the tests, running the tests, failing, and
successfully implementing the production code, the end result of the subject under test
will look somewhat like the following example.

```
package com.oreilly.testingscala

class AlbumMultipleStorageService {
    val mysqlDAO = DAO.createMySqlDAO
    val db2DAO = DAO.createDB2DAO

    def persist(album:Album) {
      mysqlDAO.persist(album)
      db2DAO.persist(album)

      album.acts.foreach{act => mysqlDAO.persist(act); db2DAO.persist(act)}
    }
}
```

Notice that the first two lines of AlbumMultipleStorageService are calls to the singleton companion object to retrieve the specified DAOs. When the persist method is
called, it uses those DAOs to persist the albums and any acts associated with the album.

Making good examples for testing singleton objects was tough, mainly because making
a call to a singleton (or static) method within another method is something that I typically stay away from—since it tightly couples two objects and makes one object com-
pletely dependent on another. My preferred modus operandi for testing is to call singleton methods outside the subject under test and inject the results.

The process of calling methods, then taking the result, and injecting them into the
subject, making it decoupled and easily testable, is called *inversion of control*.

In the Scala world, though, there are other different and interesting ways to wire objects
with one another. One such technique is the "cake pattern." This pattern makes heavy
of use of layering Scala traits. Since the traits contain the components used to build
up the application, having the ability to mock singleton and companion objects may
come in handy.

Mocking Functions

An interesting facet of ScalaMock is the ability to mock functions.

This can be invaluable for functions that your test has to invoke but that do real-world work you don't want to do during a test: for instance, a function that communicates with another system over a network or performs time-consuming calculations.

```
val styxAlbum: Album = new Album("Styx Album", 1945, new Band("Styx"))
val sarahMcLachlanAlbum: Album = new Album("Sarah McLachlan Album", 1997, new
Artist("Sarah", "McLachlan"))
 val billyJoelAlbum: Album = new Album("Billy Joel Album", 1977, new Ar-
tist("Billy", "Joel"))

val albumFunction = mockFunction[Album, Int]
albumFunction expects (styxAlbum) returning (5)
albumFunction expects (sarahMcLachlanAlbum) returning (4)
albumFunction expects (billyJoelAlbum) returning (5)

((styxAlbum :: sarahMcLachlanAlbum :: billyJoelAlbum :: Nil) map albumFunc-
tion) must be(5 :: 4 :: 5 :: Nil)
```

Some albums for Styx, Sarah McLachlan, and Billy Joel are assembled for this example. albumFunction is a mock function of type Function1[Album, Int], which takes in an Album and returns an Int. This function in the example is meant to represent some sort of call to a service, either local or remote, that will return the album's rating. Mocking a function merely needs a call of mockFunction with the types that are required, in this case, Album and Int. After the declaration, expectations can then be created—in this case, that passing an Album to the function will return an Int. When the function is now plugged into a map method call, the list of albums on the left should be the list of ranks that were provided by the expectations: 5, 4, 5.

Unlike singleton objects, classes, and companion classes, no annotations are required on the GenerateMocks dummy class. So if you wish to use the regular *build.sbt* file as opposed to a Scala build file and don't require concrete, final, or object mocking, having just a plain *build.sbt* file is perfectly fine, since mocking a function doesn't require a call to generate-mocks.

Mocking Finals

Finals have been another bane for test-driven programmers. One reason is that abstracting a class is often a strategy for united testing, since you can override heavy non-isolated processes for something light and testable. Another reason is that most frameworks also extend classes as part of their trick to mock classes. Most test driven developers use the adapter pattern to cover up the final classes to make them friendly for testers.

The amazing ScalaMock makes mocking final classes a snap. Just mock the final class in question, add the class as an annotation to the Dummy class (in our example it is called GenerateMocks.scala), and ScalaMock will do the rest. It's the same process, with the same results.

To prove that it works, suppose JukeBox was changed from a regular class to a final class, by simply adding final. All the tests we have written using ScalaMock would continue to pass. The following code snippet is a JukeBox that has been made into a final class.

/src/main/scala/com/oreilly/testingscala/JukeBox.scala.

```
package com.oreilly.testingscala

final class JukeBox private (val albums:Option[List[Album]], val current-
Track:Option[Track]) {
  def this(albums:Option[List[Album]]) = this(albums, None)
  def readyToPlay = albums.isDefined
  def play = new JukeBox(albums, Some(albums.get(0).tracks.get(0)))
}
```

Rerunning the previous test case that mocked JukeBox shows that Jukebox is actually mocked.

```
class UsingScalaMockSample extends Spec with MustMatchers with MockFactory with
GeneratedMockFactory {
  describe("ScalaMocks can create mocks of various structures") {

    //Omitted previous tests for brevity

    it("can also mock regular object, and along with other traits") {
      val daoMock = mock[DAO]
      //set up actual values to be used.
      val theGratefulDead: Band = mock[Band]
      val wyntonMarsalis: Artist = mock[Artist]
      val psychedelicFurs: Band = mock[Band]
      val ericClapton: Artist = mock[Artist]

      val workingmansDead = mock[Album]
      val midnightToMidnight = mock[Album]
      val wyntonAndClapton = mock[Album]

      val jukeBox = mock[JukeBox]

      //create the subject under test
      val jukeboxStorageService = new JukeboxStorageService(daoMock)

      inSequence {

          jukeBox.expects.albums returning (Some(List(workingmansDead, midnightTo-
Midnight, wyntonAndClapton)))

          daoMock.expects.persist(workingmansDead)
```

```
        workingmansDead.expects.acts returning (List(theGratefulDead))
        daoMock.expects.persist(theGratefulDead)

        daoMock.expects.persist(midnightToMidnight)
        midnightToMidnight.expects.acts returning (List(psychedelicFurs))
        daoMock.expects.persist(psychedelicFurs)

        daoMock.expects.persist(wyntonAndClapton)
         wyntonAndClapton.expects.acts returning (List(ericClapton, wyntonMarsa-
lis))
        daoMock.expects.persist(ericClapton)
        daoMock.expects.persist(wyntonMarsalis)
      }

      jukeboxStorageService.persist(jukeBox)
    }

    //Omitted next tests for brevity
  }
}
```

Even though Jukebox is final, running the test will cause no detriment to this test whatsoever.

```
[info] ScalaMocks can create mocks of various structures
[info] - can create a mock for a trait
[info] - can also mock regular object, and along with other traits
[info] - can mock a singleton object
[info] - can mock a companion object
[info] - can mock a function
```

The Jukebox has no reason to be a final class: the final keyword in this example is for the purpose of demonstration.

Creating stunt doubles is a test-driven development canon. Test-driven development requires that only one class is the subject of the test, no other. All other classes and objects will need to be replaced with either a fake, a dummy, a stub, or a mock. The popular Java mocking frameworks work really well in Scala, and as seen, testing frameworks such as ScalaTest and Specs2 have sugars that make a simple process even simpler by making mocking look like an inherit part of its own package.

If the test-driven developer requires more power to mock objects like functions, Scala `object`, and `final` classes, then ScalaMock is the mocking library to use.

Given what you have learned in this chapter, you may find yourself attracted to one testing framework over another either based on the mocking syntax sugars or whether it supports ScalaMock at this time, although I anticipate that both ScalaTest and Specs2 will support ScalaMock in the future.

CHAPTER 6

ScalaCheck

Scala Check is automated testing. To be more precise, it fully automates test generation so that there is no need to create test data. We have already seen two ways to feed test data into ScalaTest. TestNG covered the TestNG `DataProvider` that lets the end user create test data and send it to the test method for processing. Specs2 has `DataTable` functionality that allows the developer to create an ASCII-like table with test data that is similarly thrown into the test line-by-line. ScalaCheck is fundamentally different from these frameworks; it generates semirandom data within the parameters you request, so you don't have to take the time to come up with test data. Not only does it randomly generate data, saving time, it also makes your code more robust, because a human tester is not likely to think of the full range of values that the program can receive during real use.

ScalaCheck is derived from the Haskell product QuickCheck, and is open source.

There are three main components to ScalaCheck. One is a `Properties` class that defines tests and runs them through a test harness called `Prop`. Properties can be mixed and matched with various groupings and combinations, as well as filtered to provide only the data needed for the test.

ScalaCheck also provides a `Gen` object, which is a generator class that provides much of the fake data and allows you to control the kind of data created. For instance, if you want only positive integers, you can use `Gen` to eliminate negative integers and zero.

Finally, the `Arbitrary` class is used for custom types, which of course are useful because your programs are made up of more than primitive types. This chapter will cover `Property`, `Gen`, `Arbitrary`, and a few other features.

ScalaCheck also is integrated with the two major Scala testing frameworks that have their own special sugars: ScalaTest and Specs2. Each of these will be covered in this chapter.

ScalaCheck requires only one dependency in the *build.sbt* file. ScalaCheck, like ScalaTest and Specs2, also runs out of the box in SBT without any special configuration. It recognizes any ScalaCheck properties and runs automatically. The following listing contains all the latest items required for *build.sbt*, with the last dependency being the ScalaCheck library.

```
name := "Testing Scala"

version := "1.0"

scalaVersion := "2.9.0-1"

resolvers ++= Seq("snapshots" at "http://scala-tools.org/repo-snapshots",
                  "releases"  at "http://scala-tools.org/repo-releases")

libraryDependencies ++= Seq(
  "org.scalatest" %% "scalatest" % "1.8" % "test" withSources() withJavadoc(),
  "joda-time" % "joda-time" % "1.6.2" withSources() withJavadoc(),
  "junit" % "junit" % "4.10" withSources() withJavadoc(),
  "org.testng" % "testng" % "6.1.1" % "test" withSources() withJavadoc(),
  "org.specs2" %% "specs2" % "1.12.3" % "test" withSources() withJavadoc(),
  "org.easymock" % "easymock" % "3.1" % "test" withSources() withJavadoc(),
  "org.mockito" % "mockito-core" % "1.9.0" % "test" withSources() withJavadoc(),
  "org.scalacheck" %% "scalacheck" % "1.10.0" % "test" withSources() withJava-
doc(),
  "org.scalamock" %% "scalamock-scalatest-support" % "2.4")
```

After the requisite `reload` and `update`, ScalaCheck is ready to use.

Properties

The ScalaCheck test harness is the `Prop`, and the testing class is a collection of `Proper ties`. To create a ScalaCheck test, create an object that extends `Properties`. The following is a basic test `object` for a ScalaCheck test. The argument passed to the constructor of the super class is the name that describes the test, `Simple Math`.

src/test/scala/com/oreilly/testingscala/BasicScalaCheckProperties.scala.

```
package com.oreilly.testingscala

import org.scalacheck.{Prop, Properties}

object BasicScalaCheckProperties extends Properties("Simple Math"){
  property("Sum is greater than its parts") = Prop.forAll {(x:Int, y:Int) => x
+y > x && x+y > y}
}
```

The title is sent to the superclass as a `String` parameter. A `Properties` test must be an object (a Scala singleton) and not a class. Otherwise, the test will not run.

Each property takes a String to describe the purpose of the test. The example shown tests whether the sum of two numbers is greater than the sum of each number by itself. (Hint: it isn't always.) The left side of the assignment statement is referred to as the *property specifier*, while the right side is the actual Prop test. Prop.forAll takes, as its parameter, a function whose arguments describe the data that the test developer wants automatically generated for a test. In this example, the Prop will provide two integers, and ScalaCheck will test the assertion that the sum is greater than the first created number (x), then that it is greater than the second created number (y).

Running the test using either test or test-only in SBT renders the following output.

src/test/scala/com/oreilly/testingscala/BasicScalaCheckProperties.scala.

```
> ~test-only com.oreilly.testingscala.BasicScalaCheckProperties
[info] ! String.Sum is greater than its parts: Falsified after 0 passed tests.
[info] > ARG_0: 0
[info] > ARG_1: 0
[error] Failed: : Total 1, Failed 1, Errors 0, Passed 0, Skipped 0
[error] Failed tests:
[error]     com.oreilly.testingscala.BasicScalaCheckProperties
[error]     {file:/home/danno/testing_scala_book.git/testingscala/}default-cef86a/
test:test-only: Tests unsuccessful
[error] Total time: 0 s, completed Jan 11, 2012 10:26:08 PM
1. Waiting for source changes... (press enter to interrupt)
```

It didn't take long for the test to fail, and ScalaCheck is nice enough to let us in on why it failed to pass. In the output, the Property check failed when both arguments, ARG_0 and ARG_1, were zero.

Let's change the test to something a bit more successful.

src/test/scala/com/oreilly/testingscala/BasicScalaCheckProperties.scala.

```
package com.oreilly.testingscala

import org.scalacheck.{Prop, Properties}

object BasicScalaCheckProperties extends Properties("Simple Math"){
  property("Sums are associative") = Prop.forAll {(x:Int, y:Int) => x+y == y+x}
}
```

Running the test now reports success. This success shows how thoroughly this method was tested by reporting that Sums are associative passed 100 tests. This is very worth repeating: *100 separate combinations* of integers were tested, without the test developer typing in any data table or data provider, often times, with data that the developer did not consider. In the case of integers that can include a 0, MAX_VALUE, and MIN_VALUE. For floating-point numbers, that can include NaN, Infinity, and -Infinity.

```
> ~test-only com.oreilly.testingscala.BasicScalaCheckProperties
[info] Compiling 1 Scala source to /home/danno/testing_scala_book.git/testings-
```

```
cala/target/scala-2.9.0-1/test-classes...
[info] + Simple Math.Sums are associative: OK, passed 100 tests.
[info] Passed: : Total 1, Failed 0, Errors 0, Passed 1, Skipped 0
[success] Total time: 21 s, completed Jan 11, 2012 10:42:06 PM
1. Waiting for source changes... (press enter to interrupt)
```

Constraining Properties

The next few examples test some of the music-based code that was developed in earlier chapters, to give our production code some good vetting. First, we'll generate some first, middle, and last names in the style that we tested in `AcceptanceSpecification`. We've designed the string so that the middle name is optional, so the following definition of the property contains two cases. ScalaCheck will generate some strings with a middle name and some without.

/src/test/scala/com/oreilly/testingscala/ArtistScalaCheckProperties.scala

```
package com.oreilly.testingscala

import org.scalacheck.{Prop, Properties}


object ArtistScalaCheckProperties extends Properties("Testing Artists Thorough-
ly") {
  property("middleNames") =
    Prop.forAll {
      (firstName: String, middleName: Option[String], lastName: String) =>
        middleName match {
          case Some(x) =>
            val artist = new Artist(firstName, x, lastName)
            artist.fullName == firstName + " " + x + " " + lastName
          case _ =>
            val artist = new Artist(firstName, lastName)
            artist.fullName == firstName + " " + lastName
        }
    }
}
```

ScalaCheck is very thorough with string testing. In the property we just defined, some of the values created are pretty random characters, not limited to those in the Latin character code. A sample follows of a first name, middle name, and last name set created by ScalaCheck.

```
(ก□□□□'Ey 섷□^□□ 쥀뱇븜変칩□
姅'Hι 懷갋□ 蕣㈏□□ 댲澼□긑 릟흰烸帘攢'數□ 갦□□,Some(氷□□□□銠Ϭ□□
趼嬓□돠□ 晰□偵駘嵢□□ 옐侊霳焗□ 괇□□□□揨□ 둶攉勱枰栍삼□□□□墘侤
□□ 鋨□ لجي □,□ 趹뫋鶵鎺□ 뽧漉佯唽輕□ 鑅멻□爆령鮊, 뤓□□)
```

In fact, come to think of it, this doesn't contain many Latin/English characters at all! ScalaCheck does well at providing even the most esoteric data, which will add to the confidence level of any test. In contrast, it is highly unlikely that a test developer would even consider randomly chosen Unicode characters for a string, unless they require a very internationalized application.

Of course, that's a lot of weird data for most tests, and the data sometimes needs to be constrained to give a more realistic test set. If you know that a test requires only alpha-numeric characters, only positive integers, etc, ScalaCheck makes it easy to customize the data provided.

The next sample object uses additional Gen parameters to change the type of data given to the test. Prop.forAll now takes three additional parameters that correspond to the first name, middle name, and last name it will create. The first parameter requests that the first element be an alphabetical string. The second allows either Some with an alphabetical string or None for the second element. The third parameter, like the first, chooses an alphabetical string. The println statement is included just to print a sample of the data that ScalaCheck is creating, so you can verify that all the data consists of ASCII letters. The rest of the code is the same as before.

src/test/scala/com/oreilly/testingscala/ArtistScalaCheckProperties.scala.

```
object ArtistScalaCheckProperties extends Properties("Testing Artists Thorough-
ly") {
  property("middleNames") =
      Prop.forAll (Gen.alphaStr, Gen.oneOf(Gen.alphaStr.sample, None), Gen.al-
phaStr) {
      (firstName: String, middleName: Option[String], lastName: String) =>
        println(firstName, middleName, lastName)
        middleName match {
          case Some(x) =>
            val artist = new Artist(firstName, x, lastName)
            artist.fullName == firstName + " " + x + " " + lastName
          case _ =>
            val artist = new Artist(firstName, lastName)
            artist.fullName == firstName + " " + lastName
        }
    }
}
```

A resulting data looks like the following, which is vastly different from some of the varying global character sets. The first sample shown has a first and last name, with no middle name. The second example is the same but with longer string length, and finally comes a case with all three names: first, middle, and last.

```
(tvzoTzJppo,None,gygoprpyzw)
(OzebmzjbbovreytrmsfwuwfbsmlvjkzutwcbbfspqJhrjqqwdaveArsel,None,gbuxlswkf-
hyeyplrtzKkasfklrzkjaktygrzucftfhlfeeuxlleoin)
(zfvtoVki,Some(ggohbctymlkjsrmmprcRigdiqmygtfDmsknwcoikzbhzrfwuoNgrNwjcj-
mohcznrbzldiRcmcGscambzaporrmnc),noodpvKwusaRwzimZxujgqvknnlfgqVq)
```

The end result of the test is pure success with 100 varying tests.

```
[info] + Testing Artists Thoroughly.middleNames: OK, passed 100 tests.
[info] Passed: : Total 1, Failed 0, Errors 0, Passed 1, Skipped 0
[success] Total time: 4 s, completed Jan 12, 2012 12:10:35 AM
```

A different way to constrain a test is by using a *conditional property*. Conditional properties are essentially filters where you stipulate what is considered good data for the test. In the next example, we may want to test numbers against particularly high or particularly low values.

The following example limits the year an album was made to within the 20th and 21st centuries. Our constraints would need a number from 1900 to maybe 3000, since we may have already taken care of validating the year of an album's creation. The year 3000 was created arbitrarily.

Using constraints in ScalaCheck requires only the use of a new ==> operator, an *implication operator* that divides the filtering logic from the test itself.

src/test/scala/com/oreilly/testingscala/AlbumScalaCheckProperties.scala.

```
package com.oreilly.testingscala

import org.scalacheck.{Prop, Properties}
import org.scalacheck.Prop._

object AlbumScalaCheckProperties extends Properties("Album Creation") {
  property("album can be created using a year from 1900 to 3000") =
    Prop.forAll {
      (title: String, year: Int, firstName: String, lastName: String) =>
        (year > 1900 || year < 3000) ==> {
          val album = new Album(title, year, new Artist(firstName, lastName));
          album.year == year
          album.title == title
        }
    }
}
```

This example runs through a list of random string data, and a year that is constrained between 1900 and 3000 is stipulated by the implication operator.

```
[info] Compiling 1 Scala source to /home/danno/testing_scala_book.git/testings-
cala/target/scala-2.9.0-1/test-classes...
[info] + Album Creation.album can be created using a year from 1900 to 3000:
OK, passed 100 tests.
[info] Passed: : Total 1, Failed 0, Errors 0, Passed 1, Skipped 0
[success] Total time: 4 s, completed Jan 12, 2012 12:47:03 AM
```

Grouping Properties

A `Properties` object can contain one or more `property` tests. `Prop` objects can also be combined to craft a larger composed `Prop`. The following example employs fairly simple tests and creates `stringsOnly`, which creates `String` objects and tests if the size of the string is greater than 0. `positiveNumbersOnly` uses a positive number `Gen` to provide positive numbers and a `positiveNumbers2` generator to do the same thing. `alwaysPass` and `wontPass` are `Props` that generate tests that always pass and always fail. Each `Prop` is assigned to a variable, and each variable is then combined with &&, ||, and == to determine if the tests pass or not.

src/test/scala/com/oreilly/testingscala/ArtistScalaCheckProperties.

```
package com.oreilly.testingscala

import org.scalacheck.{Gen, Prop, Properties}
import org.scalacheck.Prop._

object CombiningGenScalaCheckProperties extends Properties("Combining Proper-
ties") {
  val stringsOnly = Prop.forAll(Gen.alphaStr) {
    x: String => (x != "") ==> x.size >= 0
  }
  val positiveNumbersOnly = Prop.forAll(Gen.posNum[Int]) {
    x: Int => x >= 0
  }
  val positiveNumbers2Only = Prop.forAll(Gen.posNum[Int]) {
    x: Int => x > 0
  }

  val alwaysPass = Prop.forAll {
    x: Int => true
  }

  val wontPass = Prop.forAll((x: Int, y: Int) => x + y > 0)

  property("And") = stringsOnly && positiveNumbersOnly
  property("Or") = stringsOnly || wontPass
}
```

When run, `property("And")` passed, since `stringsOnly` *and* `positiveNumbersOnly` passed. `property("Or")` passed, since `stringsOnly` passed and `wontPass` didn't. Of course, since we are using an or operator with the || short circuit operator becomes a successful test.

The `ArtistScalaCheckProperties` object in the previous section contained three `Gen` objects. Here are some more `Gen` methods that give you a wide range of options.

`Gen.value` merely returns the value that it contains. For instance, suppose that a test should succeed when handed a `String` of `Orinoco Flow`. This can be useful when you wish to generate a fixed value as part of a larger random data sample. The following overly simple test implements this.

src/test/scala/com/oreilly/testingscala/VariousGenCheckProperties.scala.

```
Prop.forAll(Gen.value("Orinoco Flow")) { _ == "Orinoco Flow"}
```

`Gen.chooses` provides a value in a range between two items, inclusively. In the following example, a number is chosen randomly between 1 and 52, so that the value can be used in a test. What gets selected in `Gen.choose` has to make sense.

src/test/scala/com/oreilly/testingscala/VariousGenCheckProperties.scala.

```
Prop.forAll(Gen.choose(1, 52)) {
    card => card < 53 && card > 0
}
```

`Gen.choose` with two `Strings` would not work out of the box, since there is there is no set of rules established on how to create words—say, between `Foo` and `Grok`. That is not to say it is impossible. If you want to use your operating system's dictionary (e.g. `/usr/share/dict` in Linux, contains an American-English dictionary), you can plug that into ScalaCheck to create random English words to test your code. We will see later some options you can use to customize your test harness to make that possible.

`Gen.chooses` requires values that have some sort of beginning and end. For a `String` we can use ScalaCheck's `Choose` implicit object to customize the behavior.

`Gen.oneOf` wraps other `Gen` objects and randomly selects one for each data set generated. The following small example can generate either a number from 0 to 3 or the string `Aretha Franklin`.

src/test/scala/com/oreilly/testingscala/VariousGenCheckProperties.scala.

```
Prop.forAll(Gen.oneOf(Gen.choose(-2, 3), Gen.value("Aretha Franklin"))) {
  _ match {
    case y: Int => (0 to 3).contains(y)
    case z: String => z == "Aretha Franklin"
  }
}
```

`Gen.listOfN` generates a list of the size provided in its first parameter, containing random values. This is perfect for randomly generated strings that must all be the same size. The following example creates a swath of random lists containing numbers from 20 to 60, but each list will have only four elements.

src/test/scala/com/oreilly/testingscala/VariousGenCheckProperties.scala.

```
Prop.forAll(Gen.listOfN(4, Gen.choose(20, 60))) {
    x => (x.size == 4) && (x.sum < 240)
}
```

Gen.listOf create a random lists with random sizes, giving production code a great workout if it involves List. The following example creates varying-sized lists with numbers ranging from 20 to 60.

src/test/scala/com/oreilly/testingscala/VariousGenCheckProperties.scala.

```
Prop.forAll(Gen.listOf(Gen.choose(20, 60))) {
    x =>
      if (x.size > 0) x(0) > 19 && x(0) < 61
      else true
}
```

The previous test is fairly benign, since it doesn't quite test anything and is just shown to illustrate the listOf method. If the list provided by ScalaCheck contains more than one element, we just make sure the first element is within the range, otherwise true.

Prop has a nifty method called classify that can be used in such cases to show the distribution of the test data. classify takes a Boolean value and a label that will be displayed in the test output when the generated data matches the Boolean value. Rewriting the previous example as a classified test makes it a bit more useful.

src/test/scala/com/oreilly/testingscala/VariousGenCheckProperties.scala.

```
Prop.forAll(Gen.listOf(Gen.choose(20, 60))) {
    x =>
      classify((x.size >= 0) && (x.size < 50), "0 to 50") {
        classify((x.size >= 50) && (x.size < 100), "50 - 100") {
          classify((x.size >= 100), "100 or more") {
              true
          }
        }
      }
}
```

The report will break down the test into categories used to decipher the test data. This can give you an idea of the distribution of values used in the test. The previous example used three classify methods to break the output data down by length of list. Sample output follows. It turns out that this test run didn't generate any lists containing more than 100 elements.

```
[info] + Various Gen Properties.Gen.ListOf (Random) and classified: OK, passed
100 tests.
[info] > Collected test data:
[info] 84% 0 to 50
[info] 16% 50 - 100
```

The previous list methods can create empty lists, which is important in many tests. But Gen.listOf1 creates a randomly generated list with at least one element.

src/test/scala/com/oreilly/testingscala/VariousGenCheckProperties.scala.

```
Prop.forAll(Gen.listOf1(Gen.choose(20, 60))) {
  _.size > 0
}
```

The assertion in the test proves that each list generated contains more than zero elements.

Gen supports other containers besides lists. In the next example, instead of a List, Gen.containerOf is used to create randomly sized Sets. The Gen.containerOf method takes a collection-type parameter to specify what type of container is needed for the test. All the listOf methods defer internally to containerOf for their construction.

src/test/scala/com/oreilly/testingscala/VariousGenCheckProperties.scala.

```
Prop.forAll(Gen.containerOf[Set, Int](Gen.choose(1, 5))) {
  x => true
}

Prop.forAll(Gen.containerOf1[Set, Int](Gen.choose(1, 5))) {
  _.size > 0
}

Prop.forAll(Gen.containerOfN[Set, Int](4, Gen.choose(1, 5))) {
  x => (x.size <= 4) && (x.sum < 240)
}
```

The last of the examples specifies a Set of Int with another Gen constricting the values used between 1 and 5, inclusive. The sample asserts that the size is less than or equal to 4.

containerOfN specifies the size of each container generated, and containerOf1 specifies a container that has at least one element.

 Container methods can be tricky because some collections will not allow duplicates. Since Set falls in that category, there is no certainty that any set will actually be the size you specify; ScalaCheck may generate duplicate elements that will quietly be merged in the Set.

You can also use a function as a generator through Gen.resultOf. It provides random data of the types you specify as parameters to the function, which will be used later inside the test block for assertions. For instance, the following contrived example contains a `Gen.resultOf` function that accepts an `Int` parameter and a `String` parameter. The parameters are generated by ScalaCheck. `resultOf` in turn creates the `Map[Int, String]` that is used inside the test block. In the test block, an assertion is made that that the function parameter provided is indeed a test of `Map[Int, String]`.

src/test/scala/com/oreilly/testingscala/VariousGenCheckProperties.scala.

```
Prop.forAll(Gen.resultOf((x: Int, y: String) => Map(x -> y))) {
  p => println(p); p.isInstanceOf[Map[_,_]]
}
```

The above test will create a range of testing data that looks like `Map(1029697308 -> 鯉垉펄뎈)`

If you want complete control over the distribution of the test data, ScalaCheck provides a `frequency` generator so that the data given to the test block is of the right proportion.

src/test/scala/com/oreilly/testingscala/VariousGenCheckProperties.scala.

```
Prop.forAll(Gen.frequency(
  (3, Gen.value("Phoenix")),
  (2, Gen.value("LCD Soundsystem")),
  (5, Gen.value("JJ")))) { ... }
```

The previous example creates a test that distributes the data according to the weighted calculation of the frequency. The first `frequency` method parameter, `(3, Gen.value("Phoenix"))`, gives a weight of 3 to the value "Phoenix". `(2, Gen.value("LCD Soundsystem"))` assigns a weight of 2 to the value "LCD Soundsystem", while `(9, Gen.value("JJ"))` assigns a weight of 9 to the value "JJ". In other words, you want three times as many values of 10 as you want values of 4. The weight is merely a suggestion, and not an exact percentage of the resulting data sets. Next we will classify the frequencies, so we can see an example of the actual distribution of the data.

src/test/scala/com/oreilly/testingscala/VariousGenCheckProperties.scala.

```
Prop.forAll(Gen.frequency(
  (3, Gen.value("Phoenix")),
  (2, Gen.value("LCD Soundsystem")),
  (5, Gen.value("JJ")))) {

  x =>
    classify(x == "Phoenix", "Phoenix") {
      classify(x == "LCD Soundsystem", "LCD Soundsystem") {
        classify(x == "JJ", "JJ") {
          true
        }
      }
    }
}
```

Running the sample provides the following test output. As you can see, we've come close to the percentages requested, but we didn't hit them on the nose.

```
[info] 47% JJ
[info] 34% Phoenix
[info] 19% LCD Soundsystem
```

ScalaCheck has various options that can be used either at the command prompt or in SBT to change the way ScalaCheck behaves. Table 6-1 shows some of these options.

Table 6-1. Options for ScalaCheck

Parameter	Abbreviation	Description
-maxSize	-x	Maximum size of the data generated
-maxDiscardedTests	-d	Number of tests that can be discarded before ScalaCheck stops testing a property
-verbosity	-v	Verbosity level
-workers	-w	Number of threads to execute in parallel for testing
-minSuccessfulTests	-s	Number of tests that must succeed in order to pass a property
-minSize	-n	Minimum data generation size

The actual number of data sets is specified by -maxSize and -minSize. -minSize defaults to zero (so ScalaCheck could theoretically tell you everything ran fine without testing any data sets at all) while -maxSize defaults to 100. Although these values are set on the command line, you can access them within the test through the Gen.sized generator.

src/test/scala/com/oreilly/testingscala/VariousGenCheckProperties.scala.

```
Prop.forAll(Gen.sized(x => Gen.listOfN(x, Gen.value("*")))) {
    x => println(x.size + " " + x); true
}
```

This test will use the maxSize and minSize variable information as part of generating the data. This example creates a list of asterisks with a size; if this were run as is without maxSize and minSize, there would be mess in the console showing a whole lot of stars! If it were run with some minSize and a maxSize value of something small, like 4 or 5, then it would show some short lists with a maximum size of 5 and a minimum of 4. Confused? If so, run the command in SBT:

```
~test-only com.oreilly.testingscala.VariousGenCheckProperties -- -minSize 3 -
maxSize 5
```

The result is you will get 100 tests. You will always get 100 tests. But the kind of tests that you will get will be one of the following combinations:

```
3 List(*, *, *)
4 List(*, *, *, *)
5 List(*, *, *, *, *)
```

Of course, if you run some of these examples, you'll notice that they still generate 100 samples. At the time of writing for this book, there is nothing that can be done about that. There will always be a sample of 100, and the developer would have to bear with it until a new version comes around, when perhaps that number can be constrained as we choose.

Custom Generators

The default generators can only go so far until you need a generator that creates custom objects based on your requirements. For instance, out of the box, ScalaCheck does not have a Map generator. But you'll constantly find it necessary for creating custom Map data. Custom generators in ScalaCheck are typically done in a for-loop (but of course can also be done through flatMap, map, and filter if so desired).

The following example creates a Map with a single key and its corresponding value. The value uses Gen.alphaStr to generate a string with only alphabetical characters, and the key is created using Gen.choose with a value from 3 to 300.

```
val gen = for {
  x <- Gen.choose(3, 300)
  y <- Gen.alphaStr
} yield Map(x -> y)

Prop.forAll(gen) {...}
```

For those unfamiliar with Scala for-loops, and even for some who are, I should explain that a tremendous amount of functional trickery is going on. This for-loop creates a variable x with a randomly generated value of 3 to 300, and a variable y containing the alphabetical string. At the end of each iteration, the variables are combined into a Map and placed into the Gen.

Many readers will probably be thinking: why isn't it returning a List[Gen[Map[Int,String]]]? In Scala, for-loops always resort to flatMap, map, and filter to do their calculations and do so based on the initial expression of the for-loop (in the previous example, Gen.choose(3,300)). So the example's for-loop will convert to the following code snippet.

```
Gen.choose(3, 300).flatMap(x => Gen.alphaStr.map( y => Map(x -> y)))
```

Of course, the flatMap interpretation is a bit more complex, but it shows what is going on. The for-loop is likely easier to read and makes it easier to decipher what the end result type will be. If it is still perplexing, consult the documentation for flatMap on any Scala collection. The end result type of a flat map is the same collection and parameterized type. What that means is that if you call a flatMap operation on List, a Set, or (as in our case) a Gen, you will get in return the same type. So in the above flatMap operation, a Gen is returned.

Each for-loop construction can also be compounded to offer more complex generations. Take the following example, which uses a few generators to create Map[Int, String] with more than one element.

```
val entries = for {
  y <- Gen.alphaStr
  x <- Gen.choose(3, 300)
} yield (x -> y)

val maps = for {
  x <- Gen.listOfN(4, entries)
} yield (Map(x: _*))

Prop.forAll(maps) {...}
```

The first entries variable, which is a Prop, is nearly the same as the previous example except that it returns a tuple containing the String and the Int.

 For those who don't know or don't remember, (x -> y) is another way to create a Tuple (a Tuple2 to be exact) in Scala.

The second variable, maps, uses another for-loop to create a list of entries of length 4. The entries come from the entries variable. maps yields a Gen that will create a Map of String and Int, the same as before except this time with multiple key-value pairs because we've passed _* as x.

Now, armed with all this ScalaCheck knowledge, there is a way to nicely use for-loops to create custom objects. How about an Album? In the following example, one for-loop is used to create one Album object with an alphabetical string name, a year between 1900 and 2012, and an alphabetical string for a band name. That Gen[Album] is then fed into another Gen, Gen.listOf, which will in turn create a list of these albums. The test block, which creates an albums variable, creates a generated list of distinct albums of varying size, and a JukeBox with some albums. The final assertion is simple but obvious: the size of the albums inserted in the jukeBox should be the same size when called indirectly from the jukeBox itself.

```
val albums = for {
  a <- Gen.alphaStr
  b <- Gen.choose(1900, 2012)
  c <- Gen.alphaStr
} yield (new Album(a, b, new Band(c)))

val listOfAlbums = Gen.listOf(albums)
Prop.forAll(listOfAlbums) {
```

```
    albums =>
      val jukebox = new JukeBox(Some(albums))
      jukebox.albums.get.size == albums.size
}
```

Arbitrary

Generators, as seen, can do quite a bit, but once a developer has settled on a particular generator it would be nice not to need to declare or specify the generator every time you want to use it. Arbitrary uses Scala's implicit variables and methods so these values can always be available without any added programming.

For example, say that in the company that makes Album objects and JukeBox objects, a Gen[Album] has already been established and is located in some object named com.oreilly.testingscala.AlbumGen. Using Arbitrary, AlbumGen only needs to import com.oreilly.testingscala.AlbumGen._ to make use of the new Gen. Once that is done, the test-driven developer merely has to create a Prop.forAll with no Gen programming, and test randomly distinct data whenever necessary. The following example shows how it is done.

```
property("Arbitrary Creating Objects") = {
  implicit val album: Arbitrary[Album] = Arbitrary {
    for {
      a <- Gen.alphaStr
      b <- Gen.choose(1900, 2012)
      c <- Gen.alphaStr
    } yield (new Album(a, b, new Band(c)))
  }

  Prop.forAll {album: Album => album.ageFrom(2012) == (2012 - album.year)}
}
```

The variable album is implicit, which means that it is available in scope for anything that requires that type of signature. Since the variable album is an Arbitrary[Album], if any Prop.forAll requires an Album it will automatically pull from the implicit declaration without any extra work. The benefit gained is shown in the Prop.forAll statement at the end of the example. The test block requires an album variable, and no Gen had to be specified.

Labeling

Tests in ScalaCheck can have labels appended to each assertion. The benefit is that ScalaCheck can reference the actual assertion by its label. Consider the following example without a label.

```
Prop.forAll {
  (x:Int, y:Int) => (x > 0 && y > 0) ==> {
    (x + y) != 0 && (x+y) > 0 && (x+y) < (x+y)
  }
}
```

The test block in the last line of code contains three very different assertions. The last assertion, (x+y) < (x+y), will fail. As it stands, there is no way of knowing which assertion is the one that failed. Running the example will render the test as a failure and say which arguments have failed, but not state which assertion actually failed.

```
[info] ! Various Gen Properties.Compound assertions without labels: Falsified
after 0 passed tests.
[info] > ARG_0: 6
[info] > ARG_1: 1
```

ARG_0 specifies that x is 6, and ARG_1 specifies that y is 1. That's all ScalaCheck provides without the use of labels. For better reporting, apply a ScalaCheck label to each of the assertions and give it a name.

```
Prop.forAll {
  (x: Int, y: Int) => (x > 0 && y > 0) ==> {
    ((x + y) != 0)    :| "(x+y) equals (y+x)" &&
    ((x+y) > 0)       :| "(x+y) > 0" &&
    ((x+y) < (x+y))   :| "(x+y) < (x+y)"
  }
}
```

Now there is some clarity as to which of the assertions has failed.

```
[info] ! Various Gen Properties.Compound assertions with labels: Falsified af-
ter 0 passed tests.
[info] > Labels of failing property:
[info] (x+y) < (x+y)
[info] > ARG_0: 48
[info] > ARG_1: 1
```

Here's a bit more about the use of the label tags. The : will always associate with the assertion, and the | will always associate with the label. && is irrelevant to the label, since, as previously seen, it is used to join each of the Boolean assertions. If you want to have the label come first instead of the assertion, use | :. Which to use is up to you.

```
Prop.forAll {
  (x: Int, y: Int) => (x > 0 && y > 0) ==> {
    ("(x+y) equals (y+x)" |: ((x + y) != 0))  &&
    ("(x+y) > 0"          |: ((x+y) > 0))     &&
    ("(x+y) < (x+y)"      |: ((x+y) < (x+y)))
  }
}
```

Note that in this example, parentheses are required around the combination of assertion and label.

If you need evidence of which values were actually used, or, if you need to make any intermediate calculations to answer the question "How did we get to this point?", assign the intermediate calculation to a variable. Returning to the previous simple example, suppose you wish to inquire what (x+y) equals before running the test. The test can be refactored to give a label to the intermediate result so you can trace where the problem in the test occurred.

```
Prop.forAll {
  (x: Int, y: Int) => ((x > 0) && (y > 0)) ==> {
    val result = x + y  //intermediate result
      ("result = " + result) |: all(
      ("(x+y) equals (y+x)"  |: (result != 0))    &&
      ("(x+y) > 0"           |: (result > 0))      &&
      ("(x+y) < (x+y)"       |: (result < result))
    )
  }
}
```

This is essentially the same test, with two generated values constrained so they are both positive. But this time a result is calculated as an extra variable, result. This lets you track down the intermediate result when investigating a failed test. A string printing result is attached to a series of other labeled assertions using the |: all (..) construct. Given this method, result can displayed along with each test.

```
[info] ! Various Gen Properties.Compound assertion labelling with evidence: Fal-
sified after 0 passed tests.
[info] > Labels of failing property:
[info] (x+y) < (x+y)
[info] result = 27
[info] > ARG_0: 26
[info] > ARG_1: 1
```

ScalaCheck is an indispensable tool. Using it, we no longer need to come up with data for classes. Mocks and ScalaTest are all we need to quickly generate tests and keep moving. Next we'll look at ScalaCheck in use with ScalaTest, and explore some of the enhancements made to accompany ScalaCheck.

ScalaCheck with ScalaTest

ScalaTest offers some sugar to make ScalaCheck code a bit more fluent and readable. Using any one of ScalaTest's Specs, extend the GeneratorDrivenPropertyChecks trait to integrate ScalaCheck testing.

```
package com.oreilly.testingscala

import org.scalatest.matchers.ShouldMatchers
import org.scalatest.Spec
import org.scalatest.prop.GeneratorDrivenPropertyChecks
import org.scalacheck.Gen
```

```
class ScalaTestWithScalaCheck extends Spec with ShouldMatchers with Generator-
DrivenPropertyChecks {
}
```

The following example shows a basic ScalaCheck test used inside of ScalaTest.

```
class ScalaTestWithScalaCheck extends Spec with ShouldMatchers with Generator-
DrivenPropertyChecks {
  describe("We can use test data from Scala check") {
    it("runs the same but with different constructs") {
      forAll {
        (a: Int, b: Int) =>
          (a + b) should be(b + a)
      }
    }
  }
}
```

There isn't much difference between this ScalaTest code and a plain ScalaCheck test. The forAll method in this example is a ScalaTest method, not a ScalaCheck method, but as far as usability, it remains nearly the same. What is different is how ScalaTest deals with constraining some of these properties.

```
class ScalaTestWithScalaCheck extends Spec with ShouldMatchers with Generator-
DrivenPropertyChecks {
  describe("We can use test data from Scala check") {
    it("runs constraints but differently") {
      forAll {
        (a: Int, b: Int) =>
          whenever(b > 14) {(a + b) should be(b + a)}
      }
    }
  }
}
```

In this example, forAll is used like a ScalaCheck conditional property. This time, though, the term whenever replaces the ==> overloaded operator. This test will run for all integers except when b is greater than 14.

ScalaTest cleans up a lot of the funky operators when it deals with failure labels. Previously, labels used either |: or :| operators to label each assertion, so a test could report which of them had failed. ScalaTest offers an alternative that eliminates the need to write explicit labels. Instead, ScalaTest relies on its built-in reporting. First, as a refresher, here is the test that was used in ScalaCheck with labels.

```
Prop.forAll {
  (x: Int, y: Int) => (x > 0 && y > 0) ==> {
      ((x + y) != 0)    :| "(x+y) equals (y+x)" &&
      ((x+y) > 0)       :| "(x+y) > 0" &&
      ((x+y) < (x+y))   :| "(x+y) < (x+y)"
  }
}
```

ScalaTest uses its own reporting mechanism instead of labels. The only thing required is to use either a `MustMatcher` or a `ShouldMatcher` with a compound and or or operator.

```
forAll {
  (x: Int, y: Int) =>
    whenever (x > 0 && y > 0) {
      (x + y) should (not be (0) and ((be > 0) and (be < (x+y))))
    }
}
```

As seen in the following result, ScalaTest provides more-than-adequate information to dissect the issues with the test. The message line includes a clause for each of the checks separated in the code by and operators.

```
[info] - no need for test labels *** FAILED ***
[info]   TestFailedException was thrown during property evaluation.
[info]   Message: 2 was not equal to 0, but 2 was greater than 0, but 2 was not
less than 2
[info]   Location: (ScalaTestWithScalaCheck.scala:30)
[info]   Occurred when passed generated values (
[info]     arg0 = 1,
[info]     arg1 = 1 // 29 shrinks
[info]   )
```

ScalaTest has another nice feature: labeling properties. In the previous output, `arg0` and `arg1` describe which values violated the test. ScalaTest with ScalaCheck gives the developer the ability to rewrite the test with variable labels. The following example extends the previous example to show this.

```
forAll ("x", "y") {
  (x: Int, y: Int) =>
    whenever (x > 0 && y > 0) {
      (x + y) should (not be (0) and ((be > 0) and (be < (x+y))))
    }
}
```

`forAll` uses two variables called x and y, and the names provide a nice way to display the output of the test, giving the developer a better chance at finding issues. Compare the following output with the output of the previous example. Instead of `arg_0` it shows the name of the variable, x, and instead of `arg_1` it shows y. Glorious!

```
[info]   TestFailedException was thrown during property evaluation.
[info]   Message: 9 was not equal to 0, but 9 was greater than 0, but 9 was not
less than 9
[info]   Location: (ScalaTestWithScalaCheck.scala:39)
[info]   Occurred when passed generated values (
[info]     x = 8, // 39 shrinks
[info]     y = 1 // 29 shrinks
[info]   )
```

Shrinks in ScalaCheck and in this example are minimizations of the values that fail the test. Why? Because it is easier to determine that a test failed with 8 and 1 than with 10,321 and 948. You can create your own minimization strategies in ScalaCheck if you wish. Due to constraints on the size of this book, it will not be covered.

Generators

Plugging in a generator in ScalaTest is much like a ScalaCheck property, except that names can also be associated with the Gen. First, here is an example of a Gen used for a test.

```
forAll(Gen.choose(10, 20), Gen.choose(30, 40)) {
    (a: Int, b: Int) =>
        (a + b) should equal((a + b)) // Should fail
}
```

This has nothing particularly new; it looks very similar to a ScalaCheck property. But ScalaTest lets you assign a name to a Gen, which is valuable for determining errors in the output of a test.

```
forAll((Gen.choose(10, 20), "a"), (Gen.choose(30, 40), "b")) {
    (a: Int, b: Int) =>
        (a + b) should equal(a + b + 1)
}
```

If, for whatever reason, the test did not pass, the error will use the name associated with the generator and display the offending parameters.

```
[info] - runs with labels and generators *** FAILED ***
[info]   TestFailedException was thrown during property evaluation.
[info]     Message: 44 was not equal to 45
[info]     Location: (ScalaTestWithScalaCheck.scala:62)
[info]     Occurred when passed generated values (
[info]       a = 15, // 1 shrink
[info]       b = 29 // 1 shrink
[info]     )
```

Obviously, ScalaTest with ScalaCheck support allows for Arbitrary objects to be used in a test.

```
import com.oreilly.testingscala.AlbumGen._
forAll {(a:Album, b:Album) =>
    a.title should not be (b.title + "ddd")
}
```

Earlier we created an AlbumGen object that contains all implicit Arbitrary bindings. Importing AlbumGen automatically provides Album objects to the test. ScalaTest can use the AlbumGen the same way.

ScalaTest's implementation of ScalaCheck makes test code friendlier, with a whenever clause replacing ==> and—perhaps the best feature—letting you label the variables for a test. Specs2 has a different approach, but also includes ScalaCheck support, which will be covered in the next section.

ScalaCheck with Specs2

Specs2 allows ScalaCheck to live within its specifications, and offers some slight modifications to work with properties. First let's look at a specification.

```
package com.oreilly.testingscala

import org.specs2.ScalaCheck
import org.specs2.mutable.Specification
import org.scalacheck.Prop._
import com.oreilly.testingscala.AlbumGen._
import org.scalacheck.{Arbitrary, Gen, Prop}

class Specs2WithScalaCheck extends Specification with ScalaCheck {

  "Using Specs2 With ScalaCheck".title ^
  "Can be used with the check method" ! usePlainCheck

  def usePlainCheck = check((x: Int, y: Int) => {
    (x + y) must be_==(y + x)
  })
```

This is the shell required for using ScalaCheck within Specs2. Most information about the specification has already been covered in Specs2. The only difference is that the ScalaCheck trait is included to use some of the sugars that ease testing.

The code shows a simple test named usePlainCheck, called from the specification. It also uses a Specs2 method called check instead of Prop.forAll to run the very simple test. As with ScalaTest, in Specs2 it is preferred for the assertion to use the Specs2 matcher syntax. The use of check is not mandatory, and Prop.forAll can also be used, which is the preferred way to include generators in a test.

Constraints in Specs2 use the ==> operator, just as in a plain ScalaCheck property.

```
package com.oreilly.testingscala

import org.specs2.ScalaCheck
import org.specs2.mutable.Specification
import org.scalacheck.Prop._
import com.oreilly.testingscala.AlbumGen._
import org.scalacheck.{Arbitrary, Gen, Prop}

class Specs2WithScalaCheck extends Specification with ScalaCheck {

  "Using Specs2 With ScalaCheck".title ^
```

```
    "Can be used with the check method" ! usePlainCheck
    "Can be used with constraints" ! useCheckWithConstraints

    def useCheckWithConstraints = check {
      (x: Int, y: Int) => ((x > 0) && (y > 10)) ==> {
        (x + y) must be_==(y + x)
      }
    }
  }
}
```

There is nothing different in this example, except that it uses check instead of a Prop.forAll.

When using generators, on the other hand, stick to forAll instead of check. The reason is that forAll supports Gen parameters, whereas check does not.

```
package com.oreilly.testingscala

import org.specs2.ScalaCheck
import org.specs2.mutable.Specification
import org.scalacheck.Prop._
import com.oreilly.testingscala.AlbumGen._
import org.scalacheck.{Arbitrary, Gen, Prop}

class Specs2WithScalaCheck extends Specification with ScalaCheck {

  "Using Specs2 With ScalaCheck".title ^
  "Can be used with the check method" ! usePlainCheck
  "Can be used with constraints" ! useCheckWithConstraints
  "Can be used with generators" ! useGenerators

  //This is a workaround
  implicit val foo3: (Unit => Prop) = (x: Unit) => Prop(Prop.Result(Prop.True))

  //Code removed for brevity

  def useGenerators = forAll(Gen.containerOfN[Set, Int](4, Gen.choose(20, 60)))
  {
    x => x.size must be_<= (4) and (x.sum must be_< (240))
  }
}
```

Arbitrary can be used in Specs2 in much the same way as in a ScalaCheck property.

```
package com.oreilly.testingscala

import org.specs2.ScalaCheck
import org.specs2.mutable.Specification
import org.scalacheck.Prop._
import com.oreilly.testingscala.AlbumGen._
import org.scalacheck.{Arbitrary, Gen, Prop}

class Specs2WithScalaCheck extends Specification with ScalaCheck {
```

```
"Using Specs2 With ScalaCheck".title ^
"Can be used with the check method" ! usePlainCheck
"Can be used with constraints" ! useCheckWithConstraints
"Can be used with generators" ! useGenerators
"Can be used with Arbitrary in the same way" ! useArbitrary

//Code omitted for brevity
  def useArbitrary = check((album: Album) => album.ageFrom(2012) must
be_==(2012 - album.year))
}
```

The `Arbitrary[Album]`, as before, is an imported method from the `AlbumGen` object, so there is no need for a `Gen` object in the test. This example uses the Specs2 `check` method; the `Arbitrary[Album]` will take care of the rest.

Specs2 has an alternate way to use an `Arbitrary` object in a test. The alternative way is to use the `Arbitrary` object in place of `forAll` or `check`. This makes the `Arbitrary` object the test method itself. Consider the following example.

```
package com.oreilly.testingscala

import org.specs2.ScalaCheck
import org.specs2.mutable.Specification
import org.scalacheck.Prop._
import com.oreilly.testingscala.AlbumGen._
import org.scalacheck.{Arbitrary, Gen, Prop}

class Specs2WithScalaCheck extends Specification with ScalaCheck {

  "Using Specs2 With ScalaCheck".title ^
  "Can be used with the check method" ! usePlainCheck
  "Can be used with constraints" ! useCheckWithConstraints
  "Can be used with generators" ! useGenerators
  "Can be used with Arbitrary in the same way" ! useArbitrary
  "Can be used with Arbitrary in a clever way" ! useAnArbitraryInACleverWay

  val mapIntString = Arbitrary {
    for {
      x <- Gen.choose(3, 300)
      y <- Gen.alphaStr
    } yield Map(x -> y)
  }

  //previous code removed for brevity
  def useAnArbitraryInACleverWay = mapIntString {
    (x: Map[Int, String]) => x.size must be_==(1)
  }
}
```

This example creates an `Arbitrary` object of type `Map[Int, String]` and does not bind implicitly in the scope. This can provide some benefit, because there is no need to commit an implicit object to scope, and you can use `Arbitrary` freely by creating a variable and using it in a test method. In other words, one `Arbitrary` of a particular type can be used for one method, and another `Arbitrary` of the same type but a different implementation can be used for a subsequent method.

Specs2's and ScalaTest's use of ScalaCheck makes testing and creating fake data a breeze, possibly cutting down the time required to create the data. Whether you choose Specs2 or ScalaTest is based on your preference. Overall, Scala's testing frameworks make testing Scala and Java a pleasure. May we never make up fake data again by letting ScalaCheck construct all that we need.

About the Author

Daniel Hinojosa has been a self-employed developer, teacher, and speaker for private business, education, and government since 1999. He is passionate about languages, frameworks, and programming education. Daniel is a Pomodoro Technique practitioner and is cofounder of the Albuquerque Java Users Group in Albuquerque, New Mexico.

Colophon

The cover image is Bailey's Shrew (*Crocidura baileyi*) from *Meyers Kleines Lexicon*. The cover font is Adobe ITC Garamond. The text font is Adobe Minion Pro; the heading font is Adobe Myriad Condensed; and the code font is Dalton Maag's Ubuntu Mono.

Get even more for your money.

Join the O'Reilly Community, and register the O'Reilly books you own. It's free, and you'll get:

- $4.99 ebook upgrade offer
- 40% upgrade offer on O'Reilly print books
- Membership discounts on books and events
- Free lifetime updates to ebooks and videos
- Multiple ebook formats, DRM FREE
- Participation in the O'Reilly community
- Newsletters
- Account management
- 100% Satisfaction Guarantee

Signing up is easy:

1. **Go to: oreilly.com/go/register**
2. **Create an O'Reilly login.**
3. **Provide your address.**
4. **Register your books.**

Note: English-language books only

To order books online:
oreilly.com/store

For questions about products or an order:
orders@oreilly.com

To sign up to get topic-specific email announcements and/or news about upcoming books, conferences, special offers, and new technologies:
elists@oreilly.com

For technical questions about book content:
booktech@oreilly.com

To submit new book proposals to our editors:
proposals@oreilly.com

O'Reilly books are available in multiple DRM-free ebook formats. For more information:
oreilly.com/ebooks

O'REILLY®

Spreading the knowledge of innovators   oreilly.com

Have it your way.

Milton Keynes UK
Ingram Content Group UK Ltd.
UKHW051423170824
447059UK00007B/146

9 781449 315115